Chaplain Johnson –

Thank you, sir,
leadership, your mentorship
and especially your patience.
Out of the five brigade
chaplains I've worked under
so far, you surpass them all.

Respectfully,
Chaplain Nevans

"Be shepherds of God's flock that
is under your care ... not because you
must, but because you are willing,
as God wants you to be ..."

1 Peter 5:2

THE WARTIME SERMONS

OF DR. PETER MARSHALL

THE WARTIME SERMONS

OF DR. PETER MARSHALL

Senior Pastor
New York Avenue Presbyterian Church
Washington, D.C. (1937–1949)

Chaplain
United States Senate (1947–1949)

REV. PETER J. MARSHALL
EDITOR

CLARION CALL MARKETING

DALLAS, TEXAS

THE WARTIME SERMONS OF DR. PETER MARSHALL

© 2005 by Rev. Peter J. Marshall

Published by Clarion Call Marketing, Inc.
P. O. Box 610010
Dallas, Texas 75261

All Scripture quotations, unless otherwise indicated, are taken from the *King James
Version*.

Scripture quotations marked (ASV) are taken from the *American Standard Version*.

ISBN: 1-59574-012-0

Printed in the United States of America
2005—First Edition

10 9 8 7 6 5 4 3 2 1

To America's armed services veterans of World War II—
the men and women who served and fought and often gave their lives,
so that we, their children and grandchildren,
might live free in the land they loved—
this volume is dedicated, with respect and gratitude.
You will never be forgotten.

*The Bush family has always had the greatest respect
for Dr. Peter Marshall.
His message of faith and love inspired millions. Certainly, he inspired
my mother, my father, and me.*

—GEORGE HERBERT WALKER BUSH
Forty-first President of the United States

Contents

ACKNOWLEDGMENTS

Words of special thanks and gratitude are due to those who helped to bring this volume of sermons to fruition: to my secretary, Susan Fields, who originally encouraged me to publish more of my father's sermons; to my mother, Catherine Marshall, whose thoughtfulness in preserving the legacy of my father's original sermon manuscripts made this project possible; to Margaret Shannon, for discovering four of the pictures included in this book; and to my friends at Clarion Call Marketing, who faithfully shepherded the book through the publishing process, and whose never-failing vision for this book has been a constant inspiration to me.

A Message from
Rev. Peter J. Marshall

A book of sermons—why would anybody want to read *that?* After all, even if the preacher is a good one, most sermons are usually dull reading. Sermons are meant to be heard, not read. "You had to have *been* there!" is a saying that certainly applies to preaching. An audience is inspired by a speech or a sermon because the personality of the speaker has given life to the words. Sadly, however, at this stage of American Christianity, the visitor to a mainline denominational church on Sunday morning is more likely to have to endure a sleep-inducing message than a vibrant and challenging one.

Throughout many years in the ministry, my observation of preacher colleagues is that those who cause Sunday morning naps are "head" people, instead of "heart" people. They preach to their listeners' minds, and then ignore their hearts.

With this background, why then would I take the risk of bringing out a volume of sermons in today's America, where it seems that the reading public is only interested in fast-paced novels?

First of all, because the preaching of my father, Dr. Peter Marshall, was radically different. I've never met anyone who ever slept through one of his sermons, and I have met many who said he kept them on the edge of their seats.

Born and raised in Coatbridge, Scotland, Dad immigrated to America in 1927. In the twenty-two years between the time he came ashore at Ellis Island, New York, and his untimely death in 1949 at the age of forty-six, he became one of our nation's most famous preachers and the Chaplain of the U.S. Senate. My mother, Catherine Marshall, wrote the best-selling biography of Dad, *A Man Called Peter,* which was subsequently made into a movie in 1955.

What made my father's preaching remarkable was that he had the soul of a poet, a God-given gift to make the Bible come alive for his listeners.

Consciously and deliberately, he painted word pictures for people when he preached, a style he began in seminary when he was first preparing sermons. By the grace of God, his seminary professors didn't try to change him. Instead, they encouraged him to develop his own style. And his own it was—unique in the annals of American preachers.

Dad didn't preach to people's *heads,* although his sermons had plenty of intellectual content. To use his writing style:

He wanted to grip the *hearts* of the listeners,
to help them *feel* the reality of a living Savior,
to know that Jesus loved *them,*
and understood what they were going through.
As Dad read the New Testament, that was exactly what he saw Jesus doing all the time—speaking to people's hearts:
the distraught father of the epileptic boy,
the mother weeping over her dead son,
the seeking Nicodemus,
the faithful centurion,
and countless others.

Dad was convinced that Jesus called His preachers to do likewise. As Dad put it to the students at Gettysburg Theological Seminary: "Consider . . . the needs of the people who will come to hear you preach. Use your imagination as you try to deal with the problems that are most real to them." *That* meant preaching to the heart, "getting down deep," as he put it. Which is why even grown men were often seen wiping their eyes during Dad's sermons.

My father was a man of strong emotions, but unlike some preachers who rave and rant at you until you feel like you've been fire-hosed, he never preached that way. He used different inflections in his voice to great effect, but it wasn't calculated; it was because he was emotionally involved with what he was preaching. He preached *from* the heart as well as *to* the heart.

Gifted with near perfect diction, the few surviving live recordings of his sermons have been studied by decades of seminary and speech students. Most surprisingly, his natural preaching gifts were just that, natural gifts! He did not study techniques of preaching; it was all subconscious with him.

Rather than changing his volume, his emotional involvement with his subject would usually be expressed with adjectives. These he would send marching out in vivid colors—sometimes literally, as in his famous description of a sunset:

> The sun, like a ball of fire, sinks lower and lower, until it
> meets in a blistering kiss the western horizon . . . after having set
> the heavens on fire, until they glow
> > > with scarlet
> > > crimson
> > > cerise
> > vermilion
> > pink
> > rose
> > blush
> and coral,
> leaving in his wake clouds, curling like nebulous dust, from under
> the chariot wheels of the sun.

My father's pictorial and imaginative style of preaching spoke to a nation literally fighting for its life in a war against the horrors of Nazi, Italian, and Japanese tyranny. A war that involved nothing less than the preservation of the values of Western civilization called for dramatic and powerful sermons. That is why these wartime sermons are so memorable, because when you read them, you feel as if you are right there, in the middle of the drama. The reader would have to be heartless and cold indeed to forget the description of the evacuation of Dunkirk, or the story of Eddie Rickenbacker's days in a life raft, adrift on the vast Pacific.

That leads to the second reason to bring out these World War II sermons. With our nation at war, we are once again sending fine young men and women "into harm's way." There are many American families going through the same anxieties and fears about their sons and daughters that their parents' generation experienced about them.

And those sons and daughters are facing their own fears about going to war. Before it is over, many of them will have joined the long list of American "heroes proved in liberating strife."

The weapons of war change over time, as it seems we human beings are always inventing new and creative ways to kill each other. Yet the basic elements of war never change—the horrors of battle,

the terrible destruction of life, limb, and property,

the searing agony of parents learning of the death of a son in combat,

or a wife and children losing a husband and father—

these things never change.

Neither do the issues change. The questions are always the same, from century to century:

"Why does a loving God permit war?"

"Why did my daddy have to die?"

"Is there such a thing as a just war?"

"Why was my buddy next to me killed,

and my life was spared?"

The sermons in this book grapple with these issues and questions. I will not promise you that reading them will resolve all your conflicts, and answer all your questions. Some questions can never be answered satisfactorily until we stand before God face to face.

But I *will* promise you that your heart will be deeply stirred. In these messages you will be challenged to discover, as my father did and as I have, that a living Savior, Jesus Christ, has the answers for your life and its problems.

Prior to this book, there have been only two volumes of my father, Dr. Peter Marshall's sermons published, both edited by my mother, Catherine Marshall. *Mr. Jones, Meet the Master* was published in 1949, and *John Doe, Disciple* was published in 1963. These two collections comprise twenty-four sermons out of a total of over six hundred.

Years before her death in 1983, my mother had given to me the complete set of my father's original sermon manuscripts. Several years into Dad's pastorate at New York Avenue Presbyterian Church, his Sunday morning sermons began to be printed in pamphlet form, and I have a set of those as well.

In the last several years, I have received many inquiries about particular sermons of Dad's, especially some of his famous ones from the years of World War II. These had never been published. After several people, including my own secretary, asked me if I had ever thought of publishing more of Dad's sermons, I did start to think about it. Yet it wasn't until after the terrorist attacks of September 11, 2001, plunged America into war that the idea came to me: what about a book of Dad's *wartime* sermons?

So many of his unpublished, most famous, and most sought-after sermons fall in that six-year period between Germany's invasion of Poland in September of 1939 and the fall of 1945, when the GIs began coming home after the surrender of Japan.

It seems that no one who ever heard my father preach "The Man with the Bowler Hat" has ever forgotten it. The first time I copied the printed version for someone who had requested it, then stopped to read it, I discovered why.

Knowing that I would certainly include that message in this volume, I decided to read through the rest of the printed sermons Dad preached during the war and found eleven others. I found so many fine messages; in fact, it was difficult to choose among them. But I have prayerfully selected twelve that I feel will have the greatest impact at this time.

With the exception of minor editing, such as changing certain words for clarification, and the use of modern spelling and punctuation, I have not changed the sermons. They appear on the printed page almost exactly the way they were originally typed on the sermon manuscripts. Some of the manuscript pages bear the marks of my mother's editing, where she, too, occasionally substituted a word for clarification purposes or changed the punctuation. Most of this editing took place after Dad's death, as Mom considered publishing various sermons, including some of the ones in this book.

Sometimes, however, she added sentences of her own to Dad's sermons before he preached them. As *A Man Called Peter* clearly reveals, he often asked for her help as he was preparing a sermon. One can only speculate how much of her input actually went into Dad's sermons, but it is surely present in many of them.

After the last sermon, I have included seven of my father's wartime pastoral prayers from Sunday morning services. Placed in chronological order, each of them is prefaced by a brief description of the events of the war taking place at the time, to put the prayers in context. Prayers being timeless, these prayers will not only reach out to touch the heart of God whenever they are prayed, but I believe they will also touch the hearts of readers as well.

The Tides of War

On the leisurely Hawaiian Sunday morning of December 7, 1941, Japanese dive-bombers and torpedo planes screamed down out of the sky at Pearl Harbor to rain death and destruction on America's Pacific fleet. Five battleships were sunk, eleven other ships were sunk or crippled, and we suffered thirty-four hundred casualties. That sneak attack, which President Roosevelt called "a date which will live in infamy," plunged the nation into World War II. It would prove to be the costliest war in human history.

On the clear and sunny fall day of September 11, 2001, people were just arriving at work when Islamic terrorists flew airliners into the North and South Towers of New York City's World Trade Center. Once again, a sneak attack had thrown America into war, and the number of casualties was eerily similar to those of Pearl Harbor—just under three thousand.

In America today, however, few signs reveal that our nation is at war. Though terrorism is a global issue, most of the actual fighting has been restricted to the Middle East. This is not a world war—at least not yet.

Not so with World War II. Back then, the war was truly global. Except for Latin America and the interior of Africa, there were very few places and countries not involved in the fighting. Younger readers may not realize how all-consuming and overwhelming this war actually was. The Japanese, Germans, and Italians were implacable foes of freedom and were armed to the teeth. Hitler, Tojo, and Mussolini—all military dictators—snuffed out human freedom in every country they conquered. For the first several years of the war, the outcome was in doubt. The future of Western civilization and its Biblical foundations hung in the balance.

In 1938, a re-armed Germany began marching into the countries of Europe. Nazi dictator Adolf Hitler first annexed Austria, and a frightened France and Britain tried to appease him by giving him parts of Czechoslovakia. Emboldened by their lack of resistance, Hitler sent Nazi jackboots into the rest of Czechoslovakia in early 1939.

Britain and France had finally drawn the line for Hitler at the Polish-German border, so when he began open warfare in Europe with the blitzkrieg (lightning war) invasion of Poland on September 1, they immediately declared war. But after easily overrunning Poland, the German advance continued with the capture of Norway and Denmark in April of 1940.

One month later, the Nazi panzer tanks swept over Belgium, the Netherlands, and Luxembourg, and the French armies collapsed. The British managed to miraculously evacuate 238,000 British, French, and Polish soldiers from the continent at Dunkirk, but German troops entered Paris on June 14.

With the United States not yet in the war, and a nonaggression pact with Russia in place, German generals stood on the French beaches and began planning the invasion of Great Britain across the English Channel.

Hitler seemed invincible, and the British were facing him alone. He would send wave after wave of German bombers to force the British to plead for peace, and if the air attack by the Luftwaffe didn't work, he would invade.

While the world held its breath from July to October of 1940, the young pilots of Britain's Royal Air Force, hopelessly outnumbered, flung their fighters against the German bombers day after day to drive them from the skies over England. As Winston Churchill said, "Never in the field of human conflict was so much owed by so many to so few."

At the same time, the British navy fought desperately against German submarine packs to keep the North Atlantic open for American supply convoys. The fate of Great Britain hung by a thread.

On September 29, in the midst of this struggle, my Scottish father, Dr. Peter Marshall, preached a memorable sermon: "The Man with the Bowler Hat." He said:

Dark days have come before to Great Britain.
Her enemies have dug her grave many times ere this.
They have carved up the British Empire more than once . . .
    but still she lives on . . .
        and holds together.

By the grace of God, the British navy and air force prevailed, and Hitler's plans were thwarted.

On this side of the Atlantic, while officially remaining neutral in the war, America sent surplus World War I munitions to Britain, along with fifty aging U.S. Navy destroyers. We began building up our armed forces. The ominous clouds of war seemed to be moving toward America. It became obvious we were going to be involved, like it or not.

But there were many American voices—some of them quite shrill, who didn't like it. They called for us to stay isolated, *not* to get into *this* war.

The first sermon in this volume was preached during this period. Dad spoke to the conflict:

We all hate and abhor war,
    We detest it . . .

And yet . . . I feel that there are certain . . .liberties,
for which a man should be willing to fight
    and even dare to die.

In one of the most obvious moves of the hand of God in my father's life, he was invited to preach at the U.S. Naval Academy Sunday service on December 7, 1941—Pearl Harbor Day. The December graduating class of midshipmen was seated before him in the chapel that day, soon to be commissioned and go on active duty. During his early morning drive from Washington to Annapolis, he felt impressed by God to change his message.

He preached on death, and how those who have put their trust in Christ need not fear it. To those young men, who would soon go to war, he began by saying:

Most of us never think of death or dying.
We act as if we had a long lease on life . . .
    as though we had immunity somehow . . .

But at the end of the message he proclaimed:

These first disciples (of Jesus) knew
    that human personality will survive . . .
because One who went into the grave and beyond,
    had come back to say:
"Whosoever believeth in Me shall not perish
    but have eternal life . . ."

The day after Japan's sneak attack on Pearl Harbor, President Franklin D. Roosevelt's speech to Congress called for a declaration of war on the Japanese; immediately afterward, Congress granted the declaration unanimously. On December 11, Nazi Germany declared war on the United States, and later that same day the President and Congress quickly reciprocated.

The voices of isolation were stilled. We were at war.

For the first few months of 1941, Americans watched helplessly as Japan ruthlessly expanded its empire in the Pacific. The Japanese quickly took Burma, Malaya, Singapore, and the Dutch East Indies. Only the Philippines held out. But on May 6, 1942, the Stars and Stripes were hauled down on the fortress of Corregidor, the last Philippine location to hold out against Japanese troops. The Rising Sun flag of Japan flew over a territory that stretched from northern Manchuria to New Guinea, and from eastern India to Wake Island. Except for Colonel Jimmy Doolittle's daring April 18, B-25 bomber raid on Tokyo from the *USS Hornet,* Americans had little to cheer about.

Unable to defeat England's bulldog tenacity, Hitler turned to the east and gobbled up Hungary, Romania, Bulgaria, and Greece. He then broke his phony treaty with Soviet dictator Stalin and unleashed the power of the German war machine—120 divisions strong—on Russia. By November 1942, Germany controlled all of Europe except neutral Spain, Sweden, and Switzerland. Her armies were at Stalingrad, within striking distance of Moscow. In both Europe and the Pacific, the war was becoming a long, terrible ordeal.

Today in America, by contrast, it is hard to tell that we are at war. Life seems to go on much the way it did before the war, unless you are part of a family with people in the military. There are no hardships, no shortages of any necessary goods or services. So far, higher gas prices seem to be the only sign of the war. The economy is taking the whole thing in stride.

However, in 1942 nearly everyone in the nation became involved in the war effort. Goods essential for war were soon rationed, especially the gas, rubber, and metal needed for our planes, ships, and tanks. Used tin cans were collected and turned in. Ration books were issued, and people learned to save coupons. Rationing was a new experience for most people who, except for the Great Depression years, had been accustomed to plenty of everything. Now, very little was plentiful. Meat, butter, sugar, tea, and coffee were rationed—even paper.

As a boy during the war, I remember eating canned Spam (various pig parts mixed with ham) sandwiches for lunch.

No one could buy nylons, so many women took to painting fake nylon seams on the backs of their legs. Shoes were rationed to make sure that our soldiers would have enough. Growing kids usually consumed their parents' shoe rations, so adults often wore out their own shoes. And folks had to get used to standing in line for everything.

On the bright side, the government encouraged everyone to plant Victory Gardens, and eventually they produced 40 percent of the country's fresh vegetables!

Naturally, some people complained, and others tried to cheat the system to get extra coupons. On May 3, 1942, Dad was preaching:

They resent the shortages of this and that . . .
they resent the rationing of sugar and gasoline,
and perhaps of tea and coffee as well . . .

They do not like the increased taxation
and the bother and nuisance of black-out preparations . . .

What man refuses to learn in times of peace,
    God teaches him in times of war . . .
God permits war in order that we might see what sin really is.

To confuse any possible enemy bombers, blackout curtains had to be hung over windows at night. The police and air raid wardens enforced this—no lights could be shown. On Cape Cod, where my family spent summers when I was little, the authorities were quite strict about it. As it turned out, the wartime rules were issued for good reason; in February of 1942, a Japanese submarine fired a few shells from its deck gun at oil tanks in Santa Barbara, California, but no damage was done. In June of that same year, Nazi saboteurs from German submarines came ashore on both Long Island, New York, and Ponte Vedra, Florida. In both cases, the FBI captured the invaders before they could do any harm.

Warning posters were put up in public places to remind people not

to talk about ship sailing schedules or about army units shipping out—
"Loose Lips Sink Ships!"

The war's greatest impact on the home front may have been on American work habits. Women went to work in large numbers for the first time, over 18 million of them. With so many men overseas, women were desperately needed in the factories. Appearing everywhere was the famous picture of "Rosie the Riveter," the pretty female worker flexing her biceps, under the words "We Can Do It!"

Rosie was actually the real thing! She worked in the Willow Run Aircraft Factory in Ypsilanti, Michigan, before she was discovered by the actor Walter Pidgeon. She and all her sister workers riveted aircraft wings together, made weapons parts, tanks, and candles; they became expert welders and presided over an explosion of American industrial production never equaled in world history. People worked longer hours than ever, and worked hard.

The Germans took eight years to build the war machine which overran Europe in 1940. At that time U.S. arms production was quite small. Yet, just two years later Americans were producing as much war material as Germany, Italy, and Japan—combined! In 1943, our war production became 50 percent greater than that of the enemy Axis powers; the next year it was more than twice as great. By the end of the war, our workers had produced 297,000 planes, 86,000 tanks, 6,500 naval vessels, 64,500 landing craft, 5,400 cargo ships, 315,000 artillery pieces, 4.2 million tons of artillery shells, and 17 million rifles.

Some of the changes the war created became permanent; once the women were out of the home and working, many of them never went back. The Women's Army Corps grew to 200,000, and another 88,000 women joined the navy's WAVES (Women Accepted for Volunteer Emergency Service). These women freed men for combat by driving trucks, repairing tanks, ferrying bombers across the country, and filling clerical jobs on land and sea.

The Army Nurse Corps performed heroically on battlefields. They incurred high casualties, with over 200 nurses killed in battle. Often they had to make do when there were no stretchers. Many had to wash and reuse old bandages. They even gave their own blood when there were no blood supplies.

At home, women worked as Gray Ladies—hostesses in USO canteens—making sandwiches and dancing with lonely soldiers on leave.

Everyone did what they could for the war effort. Parents bought war bonds, and children saved up bond books with stamps. Most houses hung patriotic window banners—blue stars on a white background with a red border. Each blue star represented a family member serving in the armed services.

During May 1942, the tide of battle in the Pacific began to turn. In the wake of the tragic surrender of Corregidor, hope began to dawn at the Battle of the Coral Sea. There, the U.S. Navy stopped the Japanese advance in the South Pacific. We lost the carrier *Lexington* and several other ships, but our carrier-based planes sank an enemy cruiser and a carrier and shot down many of their planes. The enemy had to give up their battle plans and were thrown back on the defensive.

As hope began to grow, stories of God's intervention began to filter back to America from our military people who were experiencing Him in their lives. In the North Pacific, the first solid American victory of the war against the Japanese came in the Battle of Midway, June 3–6. A divine hand seemed to brush back the clouds beneath a U.S. Navy scout plane searching for the Japanese fleet, just as dwindling fuel was forcing the pilot to turn back to his ship. He sighted the enemy ships. As a result, though we lost our own carrier *Yorktown* in the fight, the Japanese carrier fleet was crushed—four carriers and a heavy cruiser were sunk.

On January 31, 1943, my father preached a message of faith and hope by recounting the miraculous rescue of Captain Eddie Rickenbacker and his bomber crew from three weeks adrift on the South Pacific.

These eight men met God out on the broad waters of
the Pacific Ocean . . .

You and I can follow the same path that these men took,
  only we can do it in the privacy of our own rooms tonight
  or tomorrow morning,
    rather than on the trackless Pacific.

You can find Him as real and as powerful in your armchair
  or on your knees in your bedroom . . . if you will.

When the First U.S. Marine Division poured ashore on the island of
Guadalcanal on August 7, 1942, a series of island-hopping campaigns
began that was radically different from the war in Europe. On the continent, the large German, Soviet, and American armies slugged away at
each other, backed by heavy artillery and air power.

But in the Pacific, smaller armies, combined with naval power, air
power, and shipping made for a different kind of war. The same month
of August found American General Douglas MacArthur engaging the
Japanese in combat on New Guinea. With army troops, land-based
aircraft, and old battleships and cruisers, he leapfrogged his way northward to an eventual invasion of the Philippines in October of 1944.

Admiral Chester Nimitz, using U.S. Marines, army troops, and
carrier-based planes, would jump from island to island across the Central
Pacific from November 1943 to July 1945.

Tarawa . . . Kwajalein . . . Eniwetok . . . Guam . . . Saipan . . . Iwo Jima . . .
Okinawa—these names are immortal in the proud and blood-stained
history of the United States Marine Corps.

The Japanese, dug into bunkers reinforced with coconut logs, fought
savagely—usually until they were all killed. The marines lost 900 killed
and 2,400 wounded on Betio in the Tarawa Atoll. When the shooting
stopped, they had taken a piece of coral three miles long and 800 yards
wide.

For the U. S. Marines, the sands of Iwo Jima are holy ground. The battle for Iwo (a volcanic, gourd-shaped island five and a half miles in length) cost almost 7,000 marines dead and 19,000 wounded. No battalion suffered less than 50 percent casualties. Many suffered more. Two out of every three young marines who fought on Iwo were killed or wounded.

Arguably, the fight for that small piece of real estate displayed more heroism on the part of our marines than any other battle in their war. In all of World War II they received 84 Medals of Honor, America's highest individual military award for valor in action. That averaged about two per month. In their thirty-six days of fighting on Iwo Jima, the marines earned 27 out of the 84 medals.

The casualties at Okinawa were worse. Over 12,000 marines, soldiers, and sailors died during the twelve weeks of battle. United States forces suffered 36,000 wounded, lost 34 ships sunk and 368 damaged. The Japanese lost 100,000 men.

As the remains of hundreds of thousands of soldiers, marines, sailors, and airmen were returned to the United States for burial, the grief and pain mounted. The sight every family dreaded to see was the Western Union telegram boy or military officers in dress uniforms standing at the front door with the news that a husband, son, father, or brother was dead. Then the blue star in the window would be covered with a gold one, meaning the family had lost someone in the war. Often there was a mixture of blue and gold stars; sometimes there was more than one gold star in the window.

As American casualties grew, my father preached to the widows and mothers who had lost loved ones in the war:

God is not to be blamed because a Japanese torpedo sank the ship on which your husband was serving.

You can't blame God if a burst of anti-aircraft brings down the
bomber in which your son is flying . . .

That does not mean that God has failed or ceased to exist.
It does not mean that there is nothing to believe in.
You still have grounds for faith and hope . . .

Your husband did not lose his life . . . he gave it.
And although you may not see him again in the form you knew and
loved . . .
he will be near you in dear, strange ways . . .

As a naturalized American citizen who deeply loved and understood
his newly adopted country, my father could not possibly have been more
supportive of our military men and women throughout the war. There
was another factor, however, that heightened his emotional and spiritual
involvement in the war.

Dad had become the pastor of New York Avenue Presbyterian
Church in downtown Washington, D.C., in 1937. In the four to five
years of his ministry in the nation's capital before America entered the
war, the youth ministry of the church had exploded. As the war esca-
lated, many of those he had come to know as young teenagers ended up
in uniform. And some of them kept up a running correspondence with
their pastor. He wrote to them and prayed for them constantly.

In wartime, Washington was thronged with men and women from
every branch of the military, coming and going. Many made a point of
spending Sunday mornings at our church, and more than a few even came
back for the Sunday evening service. I know, because in my preaching trips
across America I meet them. They tell me, sometimes with tears in their
eyes, what Dad's ministry meant to them during the war. Never satisfied
that he had done enough for our military men and women, he even
managed to persuade the church officers to have a USO canteen in the
church, where those in uniform could find food and fellowship.

At the same time, as with every red-blooded Scot, my father was a true "Son o' the Heather" to his last breath. From the time the German Stuka dive-bombers opened World War II with their attack on Poland and Britain declared war on Germany, my father was emotionally engaged in the Allies' struggle for survival and victory over the Nazis and Japanese.

In the living room of our home in Washington, D.C., sat a large armchair—Dad's chair. Beside it was an imposing, brown stand-on-the-floor Bendix radio with a shortwave band. Dad would often sit in that chair late at night before he went to bed and listen to the BBC news broadcasts from London. In 1942, prior to American troops landing in North Africa, when the British were fighting alone against German General Rommel's Desert Corps, the announcer would often read the British casualty lists from the latest battle. As Dad listened in silence to the names of the Scottish regiments and the numbers of men killed in action, tears would fall silently down his cheeks.

With the fall of Tunis in May 1943, the Axis powers were cleared from North Africa. Sicily was taken by the Allies in August, but the Italian campaign would prove long and costly. After the disastrous Anzio beachhead of January 1944, it took repeated bombing of the enemy's mountain defenses and a series of attacks by the Fifth and Eighth armies to push the Germans northward. Allied troops entered Rome on June 4, two days before the D-Day landings at Normandy.

On the eastern front, the month of November 1942 marked the farthest point of the German advance into Russia. The huge Soviet armies would lose 11 million men before the war was over, but throughout 1943 and 1944 they relentlessly drove the Germans out of Russia, through Poland, and back into Germany. At the end of April 1945, Russian troops finally entered Berlin.

The nine months between the invasion of France on June 6, 1944, and the crossing of the Rhine River in March 1945 were marked by tenacious German resistance and heavy Allied casualties, especially at Metz, the Huertgen Forest, and the surprise attacks of the Battle of the Bulge. Allied troops reached the Elbe River, sixty miles from Berlin, on

April 11. They were ordered to wait there for a linkup with the Russian troops, which occurred on April 25.

Germany finally surrendered on May 7. The drive across France, Belgium, and Germany had cost 135,000 American lives.

In the Pacific, the capture of Iwo Jima meant that our long-range B-29 bombers based in the Marianas could bomb Japan and have enough fuel to make it to Iwo on their return. In the early months of 1945, the systematic bombing of Japanese cities began preparing the way for the U.S. invasion of the homeland. But the atomic bombing of Hiroshima and Nagasaki on August 6 and 9, along with the Soviet declaration of war on the eighth, led the Japanese government to surrender on August 15. The formal surrender ceremony came on September 2 on board the battleship *Missouri,* anchored in Tokyo Bay.

As the war drew to a close, my father's sermons began to focus on the future for America and the world. What had we been fighting for? Was it just to defeat Nazi Germany and imperialist Japan, or were there more universal and permanent values at stake?

On May 8, 1945, Dad quoted from Chaplain Roland Gittelsohn's dedication sermon for the Fifth Marine Division cemetery on Iwo Jima:

> We memorialize those who, having ceased living with us, now live within us. . . . We consecrate ourselves, the living, to carry on the struggle they began. Too much blood has gone into the soil for us to let it lie barren. . . . We here solemnly swear this shall not be in vain! Out of this . . . will come—we promise—the birth of a new freedom for the sons of men everywhere.

And what kind of America were we becoming? What sort of country would our returning soldiers find? Would we prove to have been worth the sacrifice of 1,078,162 casualties—407,300 dead and 670,846 wounded?

In April 1945, my father noted:

Soldiers now returning from the fronts . . .
find in the land they love the same old political gangs;
    they find racial intolerance, with faults on both sides;
       they find scoundrels in public office,
          irresponsible strikers . . .

As long as we—as individuals—remain morally unimproved,
    we shall have lost both the war and the peace.

And moral improvement begins with the individual.
    It is strictly personal.
    It is the work of the Holy Spirit.

Toward the end of 1947, more than two years after the end of the war, both the issues of the war and the challenges of the peace had become starkly clear to Dad. The Sunday before Armistice Day, November 9, he quoted from a letter written home by a soldier killed on Okinawa:

We will win the war.
    But then all will not be done.
America will need soldiers,
    warriors of the spirit,
to fight, that the hearts of men may be free as well as their lands,
    lest we have fought in vain.

With America in a prolonged international war against terrorists, I have found that these words, and the rest of these wartime sermons, need to be heard just as much by modern Americans as they needed to be heard when they were first preached. And, as was true in World War II, what is once more at stake is the preservation of the Biblical values of Western civilization.

We all hope that the war with terrorism will be over soon, but it is likely to be a long and difficult conflict. Now, as then, we need "warriors of the spirit."

"The forces of evil are organized on a world scale.
They fight against God,
   against religion,
     against peace.
They seek to promote confusion,
   to sow suspicion,
     and to set man against man.
All who believe in God, who love America,
         who cherish our heritage,
           who seek peace,
        who are sick of war,
     and who long for goodness,
    must fight for these things,
  and they are worth fighting for."

Dr. Peter Marshall, his wife, Catherine, and son, Peter John, at home.

Dr. Peter Marshall preaching at the Easter
Service at Fort Lincoln Heights on Bladensburg
Road in Washington, D.C., April 5, 1942.

More than 10,000 people hear Dr. Peter Marshall
preach at the Easter Sunrise Service at Fort
Lincoln Heights on Bladensburg Road in
Washington, D.C., April 5, 1942.

Crowds waiting in line to enter New York Avenue Presbyterian Church on Easter Sunday, April 5, 1942.

Exterior of New York Avenue Presbyterian Church at night.

Newly elected U.S. Senate Chaplain, Dr. Peter Marshall, 1947.

In sixty seconds they had launched the life rafts....
the flimsy craft in which they were to spend three
weeks drifting on the eight-foot swells of the
Pacific ocean.

The story of the twenty-one days is a gripping epic
of human fortitude and courage.
It should be read by every American and preserved with
the sagas of brave men.

One cannot read it without tears.
It is a moving document whether the author is Captain
Rickenbacker or Lt. Whittaker.

The mere recital of the events themselves is drama,
and any attempt at imagining what they went through
must end in failure.

It is quite beyond any of us, well-fed
                    over-nourished
                       comfortable

WARTIME SERMONS

The sea was a glassy calm while the sun burned fiercely.
Faces
   necks
      hands
         wrists
            legs
               and ankles burned
                     blistered
                  turned raw and burned again.
Drenched with the spray kicked up by the night winds,
flesh stung and cracked and dried,
   only to be burned again the next day.

They were like living creatures slowly turning on
a spit over the furnace of the sun.

Captain Rickenbacker described it thus:
   "The sea sent back billions of sharp splinters
of light; no matter where one looked it was painful.
A stupor descended upon the rafts. Men simply sat
or sprawled, heads rolling on the chest,
mouths half open, gasping."

Why Should God Bless America?

"Why Should God Bless America?"

New York Avenue Presbyterian Church

Washington, D.C.

September 15, 1940

The song "God Bless America," a little
more than a year ago, has become an informal national
anthem.
There is a quality in the song that has brought tears to
many eyes, and has tingled the blood of many a
hard-boiled citizen.

But as we have a way of doing in this country, we soon
surfeited ourselves with it, because
When a song is popular, it is played everywhere.
We heard it from morning until night.
Crooners moaned its words into a hundred microphones.
        Dance bands played it
                sung it
                swung it.
They danced to it.......they marched to it.......and
they almost made it cheap.

Written by a Jew, Irving Berlin, the words have a
deeper meaning than they could possibly have to you and r
"Let us swear allegiance to a land that's free....."

No doubt, Berlin was thinking as he wrote.....
of other lands where his people are hounded,
                        persecuted
                        beaten
                        starved
                        and killed.
He was thinking, doubtless, of concentration camps where
old men and old women slowly and painfully die,
surrounded by human cruelty.

He was thinking of refugees--
            homeless people turned away from frontiers.....
        denied passage across bridges that span the gulfs
between pain and pity,
            between hate and hope.

And, thinking of them, he wrote a hymn of gratitude
that in this country freedom is granted to all.......
        and there are no concentration camps.

1

INTRODUCTION TO

Why Should God Bless America?

In the days and weeks following the terrorist attacks of September 11, 2001, "God Bless America" signs sprouted up all over the country. They appeared on billboards; they were pasted in restaurant and store windows, taped on vans, cars, and trucks, and hung from buildings.

It was wonderful to see all these signs, to know that America was asking for God's blessing. But a question kept nagging at me: Why *should* God bless America? Were we Americans presuming on His blessing, assuming that just because we're Americans we are automatically entitled to His protection and favor?

And doesn't this quick, knee-jerk response to trouble on our part treat God as some sort of celestial Vending Machine that is expected to dispense blessings because we've pleaded with Him to do so?

I began asking these hard questions in my preaching in the weeks following the attacks. Like the prophets of the Old Testament, I began suggesting that these attacks were a wake-up call to bring America to repent, and to shake us into dealing with the personal and corporate sins that keep us from being a just society and the example to the rest of the world that He has planned for us to be.

Several months later, when I was looking through my father's wartime sermons, I was amazed to find that he had preached a sermon in the fall of 1940 entitled: "Why Should God Bless America?"

Irving Berlin's song "God Bless America," memorialized by Kate Smith, was a little over a year old at this time, but it had already become our second and informal national anthem. Constantly hearing it sung and played had raised the same questions in Dad's mind, and he spoke to those issues in the sermon which follows.

Now, more than ever, America needs to hear what he preached that day.

Why Should God Bless America?

New York Avenue Presbyterian Church
Washington, D.C.
September 15, 1940

The song "God Bless America,"
    which was published a little more than a year ago,
        has become an informal national anthem.

There is a quality in the song that has brought tears to many eyes,
    and has tingled the blood of many a hard-boiled citizen.

But, as we have a way of doing in this country,
        we soon surfeited ourselves with it—because,
            when a song is popular, it is played everywhere.
We heard it from morning until night.

Crooners moaned its words into a hundred microphones.
    Dance bands played it,
        sung it,
            swung it.
They danced to it . . . they marched to it . . . and they almost made it
cheap.

Written by Jewish composer Irving Berlin,
 the words have a deeper meaning
  than they could possibly have to you and me.

"Let us swear allegiance to a land that's free."

No doubt, Berlin was thinking, as he wrote,
 of other lands where his people are hounded,
        persecuted,
      beaten,
     starved,
   and killed.
He was thinking, doubtless, of concentration camps
 where old men and old women slowly and painfully die,
  surrounded by human cruelty.

He was thinking of refugees,
 homeless people turned away from frontiers,
denied passage across bridges that span the gulfs between pain and pity,
 between hate and hope.

And, thinking of them, he wrote a hymn of gratitude
 that in this country freedom is granted to all
  and there are no concentration camps.

But singing "God Bless America" is not enough.
 Waving our flag is not enough.

A maudlin . . . sticky . . . sentimental,
        pseudo–patriotism is not enough.

God is not going to bless America just because a nation sings the song.

Why *should* God bless America?
  Why should we be blessed of God more than Germany,
                or Poland,
                or France,
                or Great Britain,
                or Denmark,
                or China?

Have we any racial superiority,
  or rare intelligence,
    or moral excellence?

Are we more deserving in the sight of God?
  Are we better than other nations?
    Are our morals higher?

Are we Gentiles,
  are we Protestants,
    are we Presbyterians, any better than other peoples?

Can we show any reason why God should bless us?

Last Sunday the nation was called to
  "pray to Almighty God for His blessing on our country and for the establishment of a just and permanent peace among all the nations of the world."

The President urged
  "the people of the United States of all creeds and denominations, to pray on that day, in their churches or at their homes, on the high seas or wherever they may be, beseeching the Ruler of the Universe to bless our Republic,

to make us reverently grateful for our heritage and firm in its defense,
and to grant to this land and to the troubled world a righteous,
enduring peace."

Now it was a splendid proclamation,
    and we are glad the President issued it.
But we could wish that in it the President had called us to acknowledge
our sins,
    national and individual,
        had urged us to repent
            and to return to a humility we have lost.

We wish the President had stated openly that we, too, have our shortcomings . . .
    and that we, like other nations,
        have been unworthy of God's blessings.

Ambassador Bullitt sounded a note that is urgently needed today in his
great speech at Philadelphia on August 18:

"When are we going to wake up?
    When are we going to tell our government
        that we want to defend our homes
            and our children
                and our liberties whatever the cost in money or blood?

"When are we going to give the lie to those who say
    that the people of the United States no longer care about their liberties,
        that they look upon the United States
            just as a trough into which to get their snouts,
and not as the greatest adventure in human freedom that this earth has
known?

"When are we going to let the world know that,
   in spite of all the efforts of all the propagandists
      who call their propaganda 'debunking'
         and try to teach us to fear even truth,
we still know that when anyone tries to debunk the Ten
Commandments
      and the Sermon on the Mount,
         he prepares for himself hell in this world and the next?
"When are we going to let legislators in Washington know that
   we don't want any more politicians who are afraid of the next election
      and scared to ask us to make the sacrifices
         we know are necessary to preserve our liberties
      and our Declaration of Independence and our Constitution?

"When are we going to tell them that we want to know what are our
duties...
   not what are our *privileges?*

"When are we going to say to them that
   we don't want to hear any longer about what we can *get* from our
country,
      but we do want to hear what we can *give* to our country?

"When are we going to stand before God and say that
   we know a human being is worthy of freedom
      only when he serves the ideals in which he believes?"

We are enjoying the greatest freedom the world has ever known—
   a freedom that staggers all who will consider it—
for we are free in these days to ignore the very things that others died to
provide.

We are free to neglect the liberties we have inherited,
    and surely there can be no greater freedom than that.

I am one of those who believe that there are some things worth fighting
for,
    and worth dying for,
        if need be.

The trouble with our age is not so much that it cannot believe there is
anything worth *dying* for,
    but that it is not so sure that there is anything worth *living* for.

As a Christian—and a Christian minister—I find myself on the horns of
a terrible dilemma.

We all hate and abhor war,
    we detest it.
        It is contrary to all the principles and ethics of Christ.

Nothing we can say about war is too condemnatory,
    no language is too strong.

And yet, at the same time, I feel that there are certain qualities,
    certain principles,
        certain heritages,
        certain liberties,
for which a man should be willing to fight and even dare to die.

I cannot reconcile these two positions.
    I will not even try.
        I don't believe there *is* a reconciliation in this present,
            blundering and bleeding world.

I only know that with all that is wrong with our beloved land,
   we must show our love for her in a deeper way.

We know much is wrong with America,
                              seriously,
                                    deeply,
                                       and gravely wrong.
Her declining faith,
   her forsaken altars,
      her armies of criminals,
         the unchecked ravages of the liquor traffic,
            the oft-lewd manuscript of her literature,
            the corrupt government of her cities,
         the hosts of the jobless in spite of unparalleled riches and
resources—
   all this is *wrong*—deeply and dangerously wrong.
But there is so much that is *right* in America,
   so much that is good . . . and true . . . and fine;
so much that is worth the price paid to establish and preserve the
nation...
   so much that is well worth paying again if it should be necessary.

But our republic, if it is to endure . . .
   our democracy, if it is to survive,
      must be willing to make some voluntary sacrifices,
         and to bear some self-assumed disciplines.

It may mean doing without some luxuries—or even for the time being
   curtailing our supply of life's necessities.

We must show the world that the genius of a God-founded democracy
   is the desire of its people to give rather than to get . . .

to seek supremely the public good rather than private gain.

Liberty's greatest enemy today is the old enemy—
human greed and selfishness.

John Curran, in 1790, said:

> "It is the common fate of the indolent to see their rights become
> prey to the active. The condition upon which God hath given
> liberty to man is eternal vigilance; which condition, if he break,
> servitude is at once the consequence of his crime and the punish-
> ment of his guilt."

A columnist in our daily press three months ago said some things
that are not only timely, but true,
    and need to be said over and over again. He wrote:

> "America needs . . . a general disposition to rate the Ten
> Commandments as more important than any Eleven Radio Talks.

> "America needs . . . immediate agreement on the meaning of free
> speech, with a view to determining if it means that a bunch of
> Moscow or Berlin agents enjoying the liberties of American life
> must be permitted to work over the radio for the destruction of the
> American system.

> "America needs . . . a drive to convince the youth of America that
> the defense problem would be helped immeasurably if they had the
> same intense love for the Constitution and the American system as
> the Nazi youths have for Hitler and the Nazi system.

> "America needs . . . an extension of the drive to awaken voters to
> the high importance of selecting representatives, senators and other

public office-holders on a basis of character,
                              courage,
                           high purpose,
                      and personal integrity;
and not on a matchless record for muddleheadedness,
                           a loud voice,
                        a fair radio style,
                  and an aversion to study.

"America needs ... more faith in prayer than in telegrams to politicians, and a willingness to give at least as much time to church as to
any double-feature movie.

"America needs ... a wider appreciation of the relative importance
of an altar in the home as compared with a de luxe radio,
                           portable bar,
                     and a rumpus room."

The current philosophy of indifference to what is happening abroad is
too shallow, and too stupid to be American.

It is too selfish to be Christian.
It is not the voice of this great republic,
    but simply the superficial,
        wise-cracking,
            selfishness of the cynic.

Some of our intellectuals, in their concern for the fate of democracy
    are calling the nation back to God.

Many of our newspaper columnists are turning over new leaves in their
attitude toward religion ...

they declare that the nation can be saved only by a return to religious
faith.

The idea may be abroad in some quarters that democracy is the thing
that must be preserved . . .
     and that God is brought in as its servant.

We must not get the cart before the horse.

The plea of the Church today is not
     that people shall call upon God to return to our democracy and bless it . . .
but rather that we shall together cause our democracy to return to God
     and be blessed.

Let us remember that we are a republic under God . . .
let us remember that on each of our metal coins
     we have stamped a statement which must not be permitted to become
a lie
          or an infamous blasphemy.

"In God we trust". . . so speak the coins that rattle in our pockets.

What does it mean to trust in God?

Certainly no conception of trust in God can ever make any sense
     until we understand that
He will only prosper our ways and bless us
     when our ways begin to be His ways . . .
and we begin to keep the conditions He has laid down for national
blessing.
     And thus I come to my text, 2 Chronicles 7:14:

"If my people, which are called by my name, shall humble themselves, and pray, and seek my face, and turn from their wicked ways; then will I hear from heaven, and will forgive their sin, and will heal their land."

These are the conditions of God's blessing.

And these conditions were ignored by the President in his call for prayer to seek God's blessings upon this land.
He did not call upon America to turn from its wicked ways . . .
    nor has the nation shown any inclination to do so.

We were admonished by the President to ask of God
    "to grant to this land and to the troubled world a righteous and enduring peace."

Can we do that as a nation with the blood of China on our hands?
    Can we ask for peace for ourselves
        while we continue to supply the ingredients of war to Japan,
            as we have been doing for the past three years,
assisting its pitiless assault upon a defenseless nation
        whose friend we have advertised ourselves to be?

I wonder if the President would have changed the wording of his proclamation had he read the words of Isaiah in the first chapter.

    "Hear the word of the Lord, ye rulers . . .
        give ear unto the law of our God, ye people . . .
    When ye spread forth your hands I will hide mine eyes . . .
        when ye make many prayers; I will not hear;
            your hands are full of blood.

Wash you, make you clean;
>   put away the evil of your doings from before mine eyes . . .

Come *now,* and let us reason together, saith the Lord;
>   though your sins be as scarlet, they shall be white as snow;
>   though they be red as crimson, they shall be as wool.

If ye be willing and obedient, ye shall eat the good of the land;
>   but if ye refuse and rebel, ye shall be devoured with the sword;
>   for the mouth of the Lord hath spoken it."

The great heart of Abraham Lincoln expressed itself on this subject with saintly and prophetic vision:

"It is the duty of nations as well as of men to own their dependence upon the overruling power of God; to confess their sins and transgressions in humble sorrow, yet with assured hope that genuine repentance will lead to mercy and pardon; and to recognize the sublime truth announced in the Holy Scriptures and proven by all history, that these nations only are blessed whose God is the Lord.

"And inasmuch as we know that by His divine law, nations, like individuals, are subjected to punishments and chastisements in this world, may we not justly fear that the awful calamity of civil war which now desolates the land, may be but a punishment inflicted upon us for our presumptuous sins, to the needful end of our national reformation as a whole people?

"We have been the recipients of the choicest bounties of heaven. We have been preserved these many years in peace and prosperity. We have grown in numbers, wealth, and power as no other nation has ever grown.

"But we have forgotten God. We have forgotten the gracious hand that preserved us in peace, and multiplied and enriched and strengthened us; and we have vainly imagined, in the deceitfulness of our hearts, that all these blessings were produced by some superior virtue and wisdom of our own.

"Intoxicated with unbroken success, we have become too self-sufficient to feel the necessity of redeeming and preserving grace, too proud to pray to the God who made us.

"It behooves us, then, to humble ourselves before the offended Power, to confess our national sins, and to pray for clemency and forgiveness."[1]

And if that were true in 1863, how much more is it true now?
We can sing "God Bless America" until we are blue in the face . . .
   but unless we do what God has indicated,
      His blessings will be withheld.

The path of humility is not familiar to the American people.
Humility itself is a strange virtue to which we are all unaccustomed . . .

We have far too long been riding on the balloon tires of an inflated ego,
   and, as Peter says:

"God resists the proud and gives grace to the humble."

Nothing can more quickly humiliate us
   than for us to reflect as we sit in this holy place
on our own personal sins . . .
   to meditate upon our own shortcomings . . .
      to reflect upon the meanness of our own character . . .

and to remember all the things that are wrong in our own community,
  our own city,
    and throughout the land.

The second condition is that *God's people must pray.*
The art of prayer has almost become one of the Church's lost secrets . . .
  the impotence of the Church today is expressed by the fact that
    the Church has ceased to pray . . .
we must not wait for Presidential proclamations to have days of prayer.

The conditions must be observed by God's people everywhere . . .
  the Jew and Gentile alike . . .
    the Catholic and the Protestant . . .
      the rich and the poor . . .
        we must all pray.

And the third condition is that we *shall seek God's face.*

That means a return to God . . .
  an effort to find God's will for our lives,
    His guidance for our conduct,
      His standards for our ethics,
        and His help,
in order that we may walk in His way and keep His commandments.

We must get rid of the idea that we can adopt a Confession of Faith . . .
  and repeat a creed . . .
    and then go out and do as we please.
Let us not fool ourselves.

  We have *to turn from our wicked ways.*

And we may as well confess that we *have* wicked ways—

that we do things that we know perfectly well we ought not to be doing . . .

    that we say things that we have no right to say . . .

      that our dispositions are not those of children of God.

We cannot fool God . . . let us not be deluded into thinking we can fool ourselves.

"While the storm clouds gather far across the sea,
Let us swear allegiance to a land that's free.
Let us all be grateful for a land so fair,
As we raise our voices in a solemn prayer.

"God bless America, land that I love.
Stand beside her and guide her
Through the night with the light from above.
From the mountains to the prairie,
To the ocean white with foam,
God bless America, my home sweet home."

But God says:

"If my people, which are called by my name, shall humble themselves, and pray, and seek my face, and turn from their wicked ways: then will I hear from heaven, and will forgive their sin, and will heal their land."

—2 Chronicles 7:14

The Man with the Bowler Hat

New York Avenue Presbyterian Church

Washington, D.C.

September 29, 1940

In ... the flimsy craft in which they were to spend three
weeks drifting on the eight-foot swells of the
Pacific ocean.

The story of the twenty-one days is a gripping epic
of human fortitude.
It should be read by every American and preserved with
the sagas of brave men.

One cannot read it without tears.
It is a moving document whether the author is Captain
Rickenbacker or Lt. Whittaker.

The mere recital of the events themselves is drama,
and any attempt at imagining what they went through
must end in failure.

It is quite beyond any of us, well-fed
over-nourished
comfortable
in arm-chairs by firesides
to conceive of that experience.

The sea was a glassy calm while the sun burned fiercely.
Faces
necks
heads
wrists
legs
and ankles burned
blistered
turned raw and burned again.
Drenched with the spray kicked up by the night winds,
flesh stung and cracked and dried,
only to be burned again the next day.

They were like living creatures slowly turning on
a spit over the furnace of the sun.

Captain Rickenbacker described it thus:
"The sea sent back billions of sharp splinters
of light; no matter where one looked it was painful.
A stupor descended upon the rafts. Men simply sat
or sprawled, heads rolling on the chest,
mouths half open, gasping."

Introduction to

The Man with the Bowler Hat

If I kept a list of the most often requested titles when people call or write our office to obtain copies of my father's sermons, "The Man with the Bowler Hat" would be in the top five.

The impact of this message was powerful, first on the congregation who heard it preached at New York Avenue Presbyterian Church on September 29, 1940, and then on those who afterward read the printed version. So impressed was the Honorable Sam Hobbs of Alabama, that he had it read into the Congressional Record on the floor of the U.S. House of Representatives on November 11.

It fulfills at least two of the requirements of truly great preaching, and my father's sermons invariably reflected them both. First, it plunges the listener or the reader into a vivid and dramatic story. No one can experience Dad's description of the evacuation of the British Expeditionary Force at Dunkirk without being deeply moved.

Second, true Gospel preaching must speak to the hearts and lives of individual hearers or readers—they must become convinced that they are being directly and personally spoken to. And that is precisely the climactic point of this sermon! For "the man in the bowler hat" stands for those ordinary people without whom, in my father's phrase, "business would stop, [and] industry would come to a standstill." Herein lies its true and lasting impact.

The Man with the Bowler Hat

New York Avenue Presbyterian Church

Washington, D.C.

September 29, 1940

This wisdom have I seen also under the sun, and it seemed great unto me: There was a little city, and few men within it; and there came a great king against it, and besieged it, and built great bulwarks against it: Now, there was found in it a poor wise man, and he by his wisdom delivered the city; yet no man remembered that same poor man. Then said I, Wisdom is better than strength: nevertheless the poor man's wisdom is despised, and his words are not heard."

—Ecclesiastes 9:13–16

This is an intriguing text.
It appeals to the imagination.
There is a whimsical quality about it
and the more one thinks of it,
the more does it appeal.

But first, let us hear the text again—this time as Moffatt translates it:

"Here is another case of wisdom which I have seen on earth, and I was struck by it. A little town there was, with few men in it; and a great king attacked it, he invested it, and built great siegeworks round it. However, a poor wise man was found within the town, who saved it by his skill. And not soul a remembered that poor man! Wisdom is better than strength, I reflected; still, a poor man's wisdom wins no honor or deference for him."

The intriguing part of the text to me consists of these words:

"However, a poor wise man was found within the town, who saved it by his skill: And not a soul remembered that poor man!"

We are not told what he did.
But we cannot help wondering how the nameless hero saved the town.
How did he do it?
Did he invent some secret weapon?
Did he devise some trick to scatter the besieging army?
Whatever he did, we shall probably never know,
but we do know this—he is nameless;
he emerged for one brief and glorious moment from the ranks of
anonymity,
and then, having played his part,
having made his contribution,
he slipped back again into the shadows of the unknown.

He may have been a merchant owning a little stall in the market place . . .
he may have been a basket-maker
squatting in the deep, sharp purple shadows of the city wall . . .
Oh, he might have been anybody!

The point is that in a time of emergency,
in a crisis, he was there to play his part
and after he had served, he was forgotten.

Now, this poor man has a long line of descendants . . .
the obscure,
humble,
nameless men and women, often heroic,
often great in their brief moment,

who rise to the occasion and,
    having served their town,
        slip back again into the hosts of mediocrity.

On the Clydeside, near Glasgow,
    some of the world's largest ships have been built
        and launched into a river incredibly narrow.

One could almost throw a stone across this river,
    which has received such ocean giants as
        the *Queen Mary* and the *Queen Elizabeth*.

It happens that the mouth of the River Cart is just opposite the John
    Brown Shipyard, and, when the ocean liners are built,
they are laid down so that the ship will float up the mouth of the Cart,
    and then be maneuvered down stream into the outfitting basin.

This is a task requiring rare engineering skill and expert handling.

George Blake, the Scottish novelist, described the launching of the *Queen
Mary*.

In his opinion, the most dramatic figure on the scene was a sturdy man of
Clydeside, dressed in the traditional bowler hat and the familiar bow tie,
    standing all alone on the platform.

He was the yard manager, the central figure on the stage. Upon him rested
the responsibility for sliding 30,000 tons of metal into a river no wider than
a canal . . .
      so as not to swamp the opposite river bank . . .
        nor yet to run the ship aground . . .
nor tear away the huge chains that gently checked her plunge into the
narrow river.
It was tricky business.
Thousands of spectators lined both banks of the Clyde.
Royalty was present.

Uniforms were plentiful—gold braid was in abundance.

Movie cameras ground away—filming this celebrity and that,
    catching the colorful picture as the christening was prepared . . .
                    the speeches were said . . .
              the bouquets presented . . .
          the bows and curtsies made . . .
       and the cameras caught it all!

But no camera was turned in the direction of the little man in the bowler
hat.
    He stood all alone . . .
      Unnoticed—but all important.
    He had checked his calculations.
      He had carefully gone over his measurements.
        All was in readiness.

The bottle was swung . . .
    the glass splintered . . .
      the cheers swelled up in a mighty roar . . .
the blocks were knocked away . . .
    the great ship started to move . . .
      she gathered speed . . .
        and in a mighty slide,
          settled in the murky waters of the old River Clyde.

The yard manager's work done,
    he turned away and stepped down from his platform.
A handful of shipyard workers gave him a cheer,
    but the cameras did not turn his way.

By the crowd he was not even noticed.
There were so many thundering titles,
    so much gold braid on the stands.

The man with the bowler hat did not matter.

He is a modern symbol of that nameless hero in the Scriptures who saved the city,
    and was not even remembered.

They are both symbols of the men and the women
    who do so much of the work of the world
        for which others are decorated.

Some of the most royal personages have been anonymous.
Many of our inventions have been made by men whose names were never
known.
Take, for example, the wheel.
That is one of our greatest inventions!
Just try to imagine what life would be without the wheel.

Of course, no transportation at all . . .
    neither train nor tram . . .
        nor car, nor chariot . . . nor wagon,
            not even a bicycle.
Nor a watch,
    nor an elevator,
        nor a machine,
            nor a vacuum cleaner,
                nor an egg beater,
                    nor a sewing machine . . .

But nobody knows who first thought of the wheel!

Perhaps some cave man in the shadows of the dim and distant past
    idly watched a stone rolling down the hillside . . . perhaps . . .
        who knows?
The inventor is hidden in the ranks of the anonymous.

He is kin to the man in the bowler hat.

In the New Testament, it is Andrew—Simon Peter's brother—
    who is symbolic of the nameless, ordinary men and women of life—

who are so often taken for granted.
Dorothy Thompson wrote an article the other day—a great article—
    about the nameless heroes of the present war.

When the story of this Second World War comes to be written,
    one name will glow on the pages of heroism and sacrifice,
        and that name is Dunkirk.

Its story has about it the magical quality of a great Biblical story,
    an epic which might sometime be told in poetry
        like the "Charge of the Light Brigade."

The British Army was lost.
The whole British Expeditionary Force,
    the flower of the Britain's youth . . .
the hope of British defense against invasion,
    by every human calculation,
        was lost.

Highland Divisions with names famed in song and story were there—
    the Black Watch,
        the Seaforths,
            the Gordons,
                the Camerons,
                    the Royal Scots,
                        the Highland Light Infantry, and all the rest.
Scotland's heart would be broken again
    and "the flowers o' the forest a' wede awa'."

Famous regiments,
    the Guards:
        Welsh,
            Irish,
                Grenadier,
                    Coldstream Guards,

had fought rear-guard actions until they were back to back with their comrades
    on a narrow strip of French coast—only thirty miles wide.

In the pocket,
    being drawn tighter and tighter with every hour that passed,
        was the hope of Great Britain.

They faced complete annihilation.
    They had no planes,
        no tanks,
            they had nothing.

The only outlet,
    the only possible means of escape,
        was through a port with a single pier already devastated by bombs,
        fire,
            and enemy artillery.

The sky was dark with enemy bombers,
    swooping in power dives to blast everything in sight,
        with machine guns rattling,
            spitting death and destruction.

It seemed as if everything was lost.
    The port of Dunkirk was blown to pieces . . .
        the sand dunes were exposed to a blistering fire . . .
            the roar of bombs and diving planes was deafening . . .
                the beach was exposed . . .
                  the waters shallow . . .
and England thirty miles away.

350,000 British soldiers were at the mercy of a merciless enemy.
It looked as if nothing could save them.
Whole regiments would be wiped out.
It would be the blackest day in the history of the British Army.

The British people were prepared for hard and heavy tidings.
    Only a miracle could save them.

And on that blazing beach the miracle happened.
    It sprang out of every cove,
        every tiny harbor,
            every river mouth on the coast of England.

They came to the rescue—as motley a fleet as ever was assembled—
    tug and barge,
        scow and dory,
            yacht and schooner,
                destroyer and minesweeper,
            warship and ferry boat,
        steamer and fishing smack . . .
Anything that floated was sent across the waters of the English Channel.

Old men with faces lined and hardened with sea wind . . .
    boys too young to go to war,
        who knew how to tack a sail and wield an oar and haul on nets . . .
mechanics who could tinker with a gasoline engine
    or coax a wheezing cracked cylinder in the engine room . . .
        they all took to the sea to save the army of Britain.

How they got across, nobody quite knew.
The soldiers waded out into the sea to meet them . . .
    they dragged wounded companions with them . . .
        carried them slung across their shoulders.

They crouched on the sand dunes for protection against the aircraft . . .
        they were machine gunned and bombed every inch of the way.
They waded into the water or swam—if they could—
            to board big boats and little boats.

Many perished . . .
    many were drowned . . .

ships sank . . .
    fishermen and soldiers died together.
Heroism was everywhere,
    men were braver than bravery.

But the British Army was saved . . .
    and came home . . .
      to protect that tight little island.

They were not saved by men in top hats and striped trousers,
    nor by the men in gold braid and glittering uniforms.

They were saved by their fathers and brothers,
    by the man next door . . .
      by the fellow in the office . . .
       and the fishermen . . .
        by the schoolboys and the village folk . . .
who sailed across the Channel to save the British Army.

The little men . . . the little men from the beaches and harbors,
    the little men with the help of God . . .
      performed the miracle of Dunkirk.

Dunkirk showed the world that the little men of Britain—
    the men in the bowler hats—
      would die to save their army and their country.

Day by day and night after night,
    whether in air raid shelter
      or out in the blackened smoking streets . . .
       the little men of Britain will make her great again . . .
      and Britain will win.

Not so much by the heroism of her fighting men . . .
    not so much by the devotion of her magnificent navy . . .
      not so much by the incredible deeds of the Royal Air Force

but by the untiring service of the Air Raid Wardens . . .
                                    the firemen . . .
                            the office clerks
                        the businessmen,
                    the merchants.

In short—the war will be won,
        not so much by the fellow in the tin hat
            as by the man in the bowler hat.

Do not be afraid.
Hitler cannot conquer,
        though he may oppress . . .
            and for a time control.

Hate cannot win . . .
        Destruction may come.
It has happened before to the children of God.

Dark days have come before to Great Britain.
Her enemies have dug her grave many times ere this.
They have carved up the British Empire more than once . . .
        but still she lives on . . .
            and holds together.

We need never be ashamed to repeat over and over
        the stories of Lincoln—the rail-splitter,
            of Garfield—the mule-driver on the canal towpath,
                of Coolidge—the timid son of an obscure Vermont farmer . . .
        or of Booker T. Washington—like Moses—the slaveborn emancipator . . .

All those were Andrews—the glory of any democracy!

They are the people who carry on and support the work of the Church . . .
        they are the people who give most generously
            to the advancement of the Kingdom of God . . .

the people who form the backbone of our country . . .
    who go to its polls,
        who pay its taxes,
            who fight its wars,
                who support its Community Chests,
            who keep up its hospitals,
        its schools,
    its orphanages.

Every church must have a goodly number of Andrews in its membership.
I mean Miss Andrew
    and Mrs. Andrew,
        as well as Andrew himself.

You know them.
They are regular in their attendance,
    Interested—but not unduly critical . . .
        ready to do faithfully whatever needs to be done.

If a class in Sunday School needs a teacher,
    there is always Andrew or his wife, or his sister,
        who will step forward and close the gap . . .

They ask no medals and they expect no praise . . .
    they do not grumble or complain . . .
they never write anonymous letters to the preacher,
    they don't offer him advice or tell him what he ought to do . . .
they have nothing to say at congregational meetings,
    they don't play church politics or pull any strings.
they are the rank and file on whom the leaders lean . . .
    and on whose shoulders the work of the Church is carried forward.

Think of the Church without Andrew!
    It simply could not go on.
Think of the city without Andrew—without the right-hand men and women . . .

Suppose all the Andrews went on strike at once!

Lines of care would deepen on the brows of the big shots . . .
    deep despair would overtake the man of genius . . .
the clever people who sit at desks and push buttons
    would get more and more upset . . .
      and more and more helpless . . .
statesmen would peer through the window, waiting for Andrew to come!

Business would stop . . .
    industry would come to a standstill . . .

And a cry would rise up from the city:
    "We must have Andrew.
      Find us the man in the bowler hat!"

Andrew does not merit the attention of the newsreel cameras,
    he never stands in the receiving line . . .
      he never gets a paragraph in the society column . . .
        nor does he rate an invitation to a State function . . .

If others get the applause, let them have it!
    They have their reward!

But so does Andrew!

There is something in the heart of that man standing on the platform . . .
    watching the great ship go down into the water . . .
      which publicity could not provide,
        and money could not buy.

The lasting reward . . .
    the enduring prize . . .
      goes in the end to the man in the bowler hat!

Rendezvous in Samarra

"Rendezvous in Samarra"

James 4:14
"For what is your life? It is even a vapor,
that appeareth for a little time, and then
vanisheth away."

United States Naval Academy

Annapolis, Maryland

December 7, 1941

What a queer thing for James to say. It is a strange
statement to find in the New Testament, is it not?
Is he being cynical?
     Is he joking? Well, hardly...

If you look at the context in which this statement
appears, you will find that James is speaking to those
who make great assumptions as to the future.....
     with never a thought of the contengency of life it...

He is addressing himself to those who never think of G..
and who act and live as if they had a mortgage on time.
those who give no thought to the fact that they may
     never see tomorrow.

His words are addressed to those who make plans
               and leave God out.....
To them, life is indeed like a vapor.....
     a very fragile thing to be blown away.....
          by the breath of God.

James had many a time seen morning mists on the
mountains of Palestine....
     hovering in thin airy blankets
like scarfs thrown across the shoulders of the hills...
     slipping down into the ravines.....
floating lightly in the stillness of dawn.

And with the rising sun shouting his golden challenge
to the darkness....
and the welcoming sigh from the waking earth stirring
          the upper air....
the mists disappear....swirl away into nothingness....
               leaving no trace....

Introduction to

Rendezvous in Samarra

There is a story connected to this sermon. My father preached this message at the United States Naval Academy in Annapolis on December 7, 1941—Pearl Harbor Day. All during the week preceeding this Sunday, and increasingly as he drove over to Annapolis from Washington, D.C., Dad had the peculiar feeling that he was not supposed to preach the sermon he had planned. It seemed that God wanted him to preach a different message. When he voiced this to Chaplain Thomas at the academy, the chaplain encouraged him to change his message, if he felt so led. Dad ended up preaching this sermon, "Rendezvous in Samarra," a sermon on death and how those who have a personal relationship with Christ need not fear it but can look forward to eternal life.

That afternoon, after the chapel service was over, the news came over the radio that the Japanese had attacked our Pacific fleet at Pearl Harbor. America was at war. Of course, the December graduating class at the academy was quickly commissioned and sent into battle, but not before they had heard this sermon, since they had been present in the chapel that fateful morning.

Years ago, while preaching in Oregon, I mentioned the movie *A Man Called Peter*, and the scene in the movie where Richard Todd, who played my father extremely well, preaches to the midshipmen on the morning of December 7.[1] After the service that night, an elderly gentleman told me that he had been a member of the class of 1941, and was present in the chapel on Pearl Harbor Day to hear Dad's sermon. With tears in his eyes he told me: "You have no idea how much that sermon meant to the U.S. Navy during World War II. No matter where we were stationed—whether we were on carriers, or destroyers, or cruisers, or battleships, or submarines—or wherever we were, facing death all the time, we had a chance to get right with God, because we had heard that sermon."

Rendezvous in Samarra

United States Naval Academy
Annapolis, Maryland
December 7, 1941

For what is your life? It is even a vapor, that appeareth for a little time, and then vanisheth away."

—JAMES 4:14

Whenever my mother spoke of plans for the future, she always added—even in her letters—the phrase "God willing."

This is not just a pious cliché.
It is the clear recognition that her future was in God's hands.

The apostle James would approve this viewpoint.
For in speaking of human life as being a vapor,
    James was warning those who make great assumptions for the future with never a thought of God . . .
"I shall go to such and such a city . . ."
    "I shall be there for a year . . ."
        "These are our business plans."

Such as these do not recognize that
    the issue of life and death is in the hands of God.

Indeed, for every one of us, life is a fragile thing.
The messenger that summons us into the larger room may be
   visible or invisible . . .
      expected or unexpected . . .
         the summons is just as imperative!

A matter of seconds and yards . . .
   that was all that was between you and a crash out on the highway the
other day.

A tiny microbe—so small that your naked eye could not see it . . .
   has called many a man away from the broken toys of this life.

History is filled with dramatic illustrations of the fragility of life . . .
   and the unexpectedness with which the summons may come.

Perhaps no illustration is more vivid than the Hindenburg disaster in 1937
as it was described by Dale Harrison of the Associated Press.

It was the afternoon of May the sixth.
   Lightning lashed the sullen clouds . . .
      thunder clumped up and down the skies . . .
         Rain fell . . .
            it was a dismal evening.

Out of the East floated the silver Hindenburg . . .
   like a graceful cigar . . .
Germany's pride—a haughty triumph over Nature.

For though the thunder clapped and the lightning snapped viciously,
   the silver thing rode softly on . . .
      unperturbed and unharmed.

She was late . . . many hours late . . .
   for the weather was bad . . . and she was cautious.
Better late than never.

Kenneled thunder growled behind the clouds . . .
   The silver ship's engines spat defiance.

Men and women waited at Lakehurst—impatient . . .
   They were anxious for the Hindenburg to come down . . .
      for they were going to London for the coronation.

The Hindenburg lazed along—
   let the storm diminish,
      let the wind die down . . .
         then she would come down.
No need to hurry.

There were 99 human beings on board.

The lightning—
   weary of futile lancing at the silver stranger—
      wandered away.
The thunder crawled off . . . grumbling.
   The rain became desultory . . .
      The clouds broke ranks.

The Hindenburg began talking:
   "All is well"—she said over her radio, "I am coming down."
      She was the mistress of the sky.

On the ground loitered newsmen and photographers . . .
   movie cameramen and field officials.

It was beginning to be a dull thing for them to cover a Hindenburg
arrival—
   nothing had ever happened.

The Hindenburg pointed her nose at the ground.
   From her sleek sides threads of rope dangled,
      reaching for the handclasp of the ground crew.

Rain still fell, but softly now . . . it touched the silken lady tenderly—
    like the kiss to one who is about to die.

Passengers poked laughing faces from cabin windows . . .
    Some waved handkerchiefs.
        There were children at those windows too.

She dipped majestically—the haughty airship of silk . . .
                            and steel . . .
                                and dangerous gas.
It was 6:23 pm.
From somewhere jumped a spark—
    a tiny spark,
        so small you could hardly see it . . .
Just a *tiny* spark...
    and in less time than it takes to tell . . . she exploded!

Flames leaped from her middle—flames of red
                            and yellow
                                wrapped in black and purple smoke.
She hung there for an instant—as though reluctant to die.

From the flaming ship bodies dropped.
    It was forty
            fifty
                or one hundred feet to the ground.

No one knew exactly how far it was—
    it is difficult to be mathematical
        when men and women go screaming to their death.

On the ground there were shouts to the ground crew:
                                "Run for your lives!"
Men and women dropped, like flaming torches
    or like sparks, with the indifferent rain.

Some of them lay where they fell, forever still.
    Others incredibly rose up
        and staggered away.

Many came through it safely . . . 63 escaped . . .
                    however incredible it seems . . .
63 emerged alive—scorched
                burned
            shocked
        speechless
    horrified . . .
    but alive.

A fool would call it "luck."

What shall we call it? 36 people died—in an instant.

At the last there was a feeble flame.
    It crawled skyward and lost itself in the blackness of the night.

Yes, James, life is a vapor which disappears
                    slips from our grasp
                all in an instant.

But most of us never think of death or dying.
    We act as if we had a long lease on life . . .
        as though we had immunity somehow . . .
            as though that cold and clammy hand would never be laid on our
            hearts . . .
        or the shrouds of that dread messenger never brush against us.

It is a foolish attitude to take about an inevitability.
    For death is life's greatest, perhaps its only certainty.

They betray not only their fear, but also their ignorance who say,

"Let's not talk about death or dying.
      Let's talk of something more pleasant."

Of course, that is true to our modern pattern.
We are not willing to face any unpleasantness,
      and when we are presented with facts which we don't like to hear,
            we call them propaganda and dismiss them.

But what is there to fear?
What contemplation could possibly be more pleasant
      than what awaits us after death?

Here we have pain—and partings
                          tears and tragedies
                          work and weariness
                                heartaches—disillusionments.

We grow old . . . our eyes dimming . . . hair graying . . .
Desperately we try to camouflage the betraying years.

I assure you that the life to come is infinitely more pleasant to contemplate
than any of that.

It is more pleasant than reading our daily papers
      with their stories of crime and human wickedness,
            cruelty and violence,
                  sordid tales of passion and greed.

It is more pleasant than the thought of atomic warfare.

For, if the Bible is true and Christ has not deceived us,
      there awaits just behind the curtain a life that will never end,
                          a life of beauty and peace and love . . .
                  a life of reunion with loved ones,
            a life to be lived in the very presence of God.

There will be no more pain,
    no more sorrow, nor tears,
        nor crying,
            nor parting,
                nor death any more.

Age shall not weary, nor the years condemn.
We shall enter into that for which we were created.
It shall be journey's end for the heart and all its hopes.

And yet there are those among us whose action—
    let us eat, drink, and be merry, for tomorrow we die—
        suggest that they believe in no life hereafter.

There never was a time when the conviction of immortality was more needed
    than in this day when materialism has so exalted present life
        as to make it all-important.

People whose vision of death is earthbound remind me of the caterpillar
    crawling along the warm earth,
        imagining that heaven for him would be endless rows of cabbage!

Then one day a second caterpillar with a more philosophical turn of mind would say to his friend:

> "You know, I have been thinking that some day you and I will no longer have to crawl along the ground, but might even fly over that fence. And what is more, that then we would not be puncturing cabbage leaves with our neat little holes and stuffing ourselves full of green stuff, but we might be sipping dew and living on honey."

His friend,
    an impressive, hairy length of green balloon tires and legs,

would fasten on him with incredulous beady eyes,
    and wonder what could possibly be the matter.

He might say: "I knew this night life would get you."

Or, solicitously he might say:
    "Poor old chap, you have been working too hard lately.
      You are just cracking under the strain."

And when the time comes for him to "die," they gather round—
    his caterpillar friends—
      and, moaning, extol his virtues.
"He was a connoisseur of cabbage.
    He was a good, old caterpillar—
      now he lies there,
        and this is the end."

And he is buried in a shroud—
    a chrysalis shroud that spins upon the twig, a shriveled, dry grave.

And yet, by and by, on a summer morning,
    the grave bursts open,
      the chrysalis breaks,
        and out of it emerges a moist, trembling, lovely thing
          that hoists into the fragrant air delicate sails of beauty.

As it dries and gathers strength,
    the butterfly becomes aware of a new world.

And when the gossamer wings are dry and their colors are fast,
    the butterfly takes off,
      and fluttering,
        sails over the fence to kiss the roses.

In our superior wisdom, we know which caterpillar is right.

We know that he goes to sleep a caterpillar and wakes up a butterfly.

But do we know as much about our own beautiful destinies after the long sleep?

There are none on whom the Grim Reaper will not call.
Death does come to the Archbishop,
   to the king in his palace,
      the beggar by the roadside,
         and the rat in his hole.

But persons are not blown out like candles in the wind.
Infinity surrounds us.
Is it dead?
   Is it empty?
      Is it a shivering void in which there is nothing that lives?
Is it a cold space into which we are launched to be evaporated and to disappear?

So we ask our questions and demand our answers.
Do we think our transformation will be any less beautiful and startling
   than that of the caterpillar into the butterfly?
We have the witness of Personality—
   the sense of Identity greater than the universe.

We are aware of a star . . .
   We cannot conceive of a star being aware of us.

We know that we are here for a reason,
   otherwise earth would become a mere picture house,
      and life the stupid walking to and fro of shadows on a screen . . .
and religion would then be a silly symphony of jazz music played by deathbeds
   to keep idiots quiet . . .
a symphony of pleasant sounds

to dull the jangled nerves of them that are about to plunge off into nothingness.

You can stand before a glass case in the anthropology wing of any good
museum
    and see laid out in a row of saucers the constituent elements of the
human body.

There is so much phosphorus
                    so much silicon
                        iron
                    carbon
                lime
water and so forth . . .
Enough iron, I believe, to make a half dozen ten penny nails . . .
Enough lime to whitewash an ordinary chicken coop . . .
Enough phosphorus to tip the heads of a thousand matches . . .
    and so on.

There, they will tell you is the human body—there you are!

What? There you are!
    There I am? No!
That may be my body—
                    it is not I.
That may be the house in which I lived,
                        but it is not the tenant.

The physicists and anatomists tell us that the cell tissue and structure of the
body changes every seven or eight years—
                            is completely rebuilt,
                            recreated.

So "you" are not your body—
    for you are the same individual who has seen several such cycles—

yet you remain the same person conscious of continuous existence.

Nor are "you" your brain.
Your brain cells change in every cycle of reconstruction.
Then how does it happen that
    I remember what I thought and did and said
        with the old vanished brain of 20 years ago?

My memory tells me that I am the same "I" in spite of all those changes to
my brain.

Parts of the body—a finger, an arm, a leg—may be amputated.
Yet the person, the "I," is still there.
The violin is laid down some day . . .
The old refrains that skillful hands had stroked from its heart are heard no
more—but the musician is still alive.

No half-mad eternal humorist tossed the world aloft
    and left its destiny to chance . . .
No infinite juggler threw into space the balls of his creation
    and walked away heedless of where they fell . . .

No blind groper among matter in the mists of creation
    let a handful of dust trickle through his fingers
        to fall in a shower of sparks, and turn into stars.

"The meek shall inherit the earth," Christ said,
    but He did not mean six feet of it—not a hole in the ground.

The grave is not their final heritage.
There are a thousand insane things easier to believe than these.

Human personality will survive.
It must survive,
    else God would be the capricious joker in the universe,

who created toys in His own image so that He might break them . . .
 laugh at their disfigurements . . .
  and sweep them into the garbage cans of His own caprice.

To believe this would make life a jumbled mystery,
 aimless and futile . . .
  human effort a farce
   human hope a mockery
    and human sorrow the cue for the crackling laughter
     of insane gods . . .

Yet where can we find the reassurance the heart seeks?

Let us honestly face the fact that all the arguments—philosophical and
otherwise,
     Analogies—however close and persuasive,
    Testimony—all of it that research can so far produce,
   are still not conclusive evidence for immortality.
They leave us in the twilight of an excruciating uncertainty.

The only proof—
 the final convincing proof—
  is to be found in Jesus Christ.

In Him is all the authority needed to garrison your heart
 when the waters threaten to engulf
  and the darkness closes in.

How?
Because He has proved,
    and stands ready to prove,
that what we can experience with our five senses is not the only reality,
 indeed, is far less real than the actualities in the realm of the Spirit.

It was through His resurrection that Christ demonstrated this to His first
disciples.

These men and women had not expected Christ to rise from the dead.
When His battered body was taken down from the Cross,
    their hopes and dreams had already died with Him.

For He had said that He was God incarnate in human flesh.
Surely God cannot die . . .
    and the fact was that He was *dead*.

Therefore, when the news came 36 hours later that His body was gone,
    that He had been seen alive,
        they were shocked, bewildered.
At first, they flatly refused to credit such an idle tale.

But then, one by one,
    and finally in groups they saw and experienced His presence for themselves,
        and were forced to believe that Christ was indeed alive.

It was unaccountable, but stupendous!
What else in life mattered beside news like that!

So they shouted it across continents,
    blazoned it over land and sea,
        cried it, sang it, preached it, exulted in it.

Read the flaming words of those first preachers in the "Acts of the Apostles,"
    and you will see that the "good news" of apostolic preaching
        was not Jesus' life—but His death;
            not His ethic—but His resurrection.

These first disciples knew that human personality will survive . . .
    because One who went into the grave and beyond, had come back to
say:

"Whosoever believeth in Me shall not perish
                        but have eternal life . . ."

"Because I live, ye shall live also."
"Whosoever liveth and believeth in Me shall never die."

But then,
    when we go beyond Christ's ringing assurances,
      we are somewhat startled to find that
He does not give us more details of what we can expect behind the curtain.

I am convinced that His reticence is based not on either lack of knowledge
    or on His disinclination to tell us
      but on our lack of capacity to receive it.

How would you describe to a deaf mute the Fifth Symphony . . .
        or the sound of rain pattering down . . .
    or a birdsong?

Have you ever tried describing a sunset to someone born blind?
    How would you begin?

Then, how could Jesus have conveyed to us the reality that lies ahead of us
    when there is no analogy within the range of our knowledge?

He invited us rather to a different sort of proof,
    to the extraordinary adventure of entering into immortality for ourselves
      here and now,
        by experiencing—
          even as did those first disciples—
            the fact of His aliveness.
For, don't you see that no fishermen and tax collectors and housewives—
    no matter how persuasive—
      could ever have won converts to Christianity merely on their say-so?

What happened was that an increasing number of men and women
    themselves met Jesus Christ.

Yes, this can happen today, too.
Yes, it has happened to me—and to many another.

And this—only this—is the final proof of immortality.

An old legend tells of a merchant in Baghdad
    who one day sent his servant to the market.
Before long the servant came back,
        white and trembling,
            and in great agitation said to his master:

"Down in the market place I was jostled by a woman in the crowd,
        and when I turned around I saw it was Death that jostled me.
            She looked at me and made a threatening gesture.

Master, please lend me your horse,
        for I must hasten away to avoid her.
I will ride to Samarra,
        and there I will hide,
            and Death will not find me."

The merchant lent him his horse,
        and the servant galloped away in great haste.

Later, the merchant went down to the market place,
        and saw Death standing in the crowd.
He went over to her and asked,
        "Why did you frighten my servant this morning?
            Why did you make a threatening gesture?"
"That was not a threatening gesture," Death said.
"It was only a start of surprise.
I was astonished to see him in Baghdad,
        for I have an appointment with him tonight in Samarra."

Each of us has an appointment in Samarra.
But that is cause for rejoicing—
                                   not for fear,
provided we have put our trust in Him who alone holds the keys of life and
death.

For at last, each of us comes back to the strongest argument of all—
    the Love that in earth's greatest Mystery,
        clothed itself in clay like our own
and dying, left the low door of the grave unlatched,
    so that God could come into our sorrows . . .
        so that a loving Father could speak to the earth's dumb anguish
            of the Glorious Day beyond our dying sun.

Why Does God Permit War?

New York Avenue Presbyterian Church
Washington, D.C.

May 3, 1942

James 4:1
"From whence comes wars and fightings among you?
come they not hence, even of your lusts that war
in your members?"

In their attitude and in their thinking with regard
to war, people usually follow one of two lines....

First, they tend to discuss the whole question apart
from God, as if God had nothing to do with it
and were not interested in it at all.

They look at the whole problem from man's point of view.
The subject is approached from the human angle.....
and the causes of war are traced in history
analyzed logically
considered philosophically
and denounced vehemently.

There are those who can show how every war has been
brought about by the lust for power and for conquest....
or the greed of imperialism
or the dreams of ambitious men
or for some economic reason that drives the "have-not"
nations into the desperate expedient of war.

The whole problem is then discussed in terms of
geo-politics
economics
and philosophy

The pacifism which has characterized American education
in the last two decades is a good illustration of this
tendency, because for the most part it grew out of
abstract philosophy......
and not out of any Christian conviction.

On the rostrum
the lecture platform
and in the class room, pacifists
preached and pleaded.

They conducted an academic discussion, not as
convicted Christians......

57

INTRODUCTION TO

Why Does God Permit War?

By the date of this sermon, America had been at war for six months, and there were few reasons for optimism. Japan's march through the South Pacific had been virtually unimpeded, and the entire European continent as far east as the Volga River lay under the heel of the Nazi boot. The Allies were slugging it out with General Rommel's tough panzers in the North African deserts. In spite of Jimmy Doolittle's daring B-25 raid on Tokyo in April, the first major American victory over the Japanese navy at Midway was over a month away. Things were bleak. This was going to be a long and bitterly contested war.

The question that makes up the title of this sermon is one of the age-old questions of the human race: Why does God permit war? Why do horrible things happen to good people? Why does God allow human beings to slaughter one another? Ever since Cain slew Abel, human beings have been screaming these questions heavenward.

There *are* answers—real answers—but they're not always the answers we are looking for. In the midst of life's woes, at those moments when all seems totally black, God offers us one hugely important answer in response to all our questions—Himself. The universe *does* have meaning, because its Creator is a God of both justice and mercy who punishes sin and evil and thereby redeems His children from their grip. The loving and innocent Savior, choosing to be crucified on Calvary's Cross as a payment for sin, is proof that God means business on this issue. God *is* working His purposes out, even through wars. He has answers for us, but we must draw near to Him, and learn to trust Him in order to discover them.

Why Does God Permit War?

New York Avenue Presbyterian Church
Washington, D.C.
May 3, 1942

From whence comes wars and fightings among you? Come they not hence,
even of your lusts that war in your members?"

—JAMES 4:1

In their attitude and in their thinking with regard to war,
people usually follow one of two lines . . .

First, they tend to discuss the whole question apart from God,
as if God had nothing to do with it
and was not interested in it at all.

They look at the whole problem from man's point of view.
The subject is approached from the human angle . . .
and the causes of war are traced in history,
analyzed logically,
considered philosophically,
and denounced vehemently.

There are those who can show how every war has been brought about
by the lust for power and for conquest . . .

or the greed of imperialism,
    or the dreams of ambitious men,
        or for some economic reason
that drives the "have-not" nations into the desperate expedient of war.

The whole problem is then discussed in terms of geopolitics,
                          economics,
                             and philosophy.

The pacifism which has characterized American education in the last two decades is a good illustration of this tendency,
    because for the most part it grew out of abstract philosophy . . .
        and not out of any Christian conviction.

On the rostrum,
    the lecture platform,
      and in the classroom
        pacifists preached and pleaded.

They conducted an academic discussion, not as convicted Christians . . .
but as thinkers . . . idealistic,
              humanitarian,
                  displaying admirable qualities of mind and heart,
but with no conviction regarding God.

They were pacifists who were not Christians at all . . .
they were facing the whole matter on the human level as a human problem.

The second tendency is to discuss the whole question from God's point of view . . .
    on the level of theology . . .
      as if man had nothing at all to do with it . . .
as if war was merely an attacking gambit of the Master Thinker
    who moves the nations on the chess board of Providence,
      prepared to lose a few pawns to obtain a check-mate.

Surely one fact emerges more and more clearly from the fog of our involvement in this titanic struggle of the nations . . .
and that is that we Americans cannot escape our share of the blame for what has come to pass.

President Woodrow Wilson told this country that its refusal to enter the World Court and the League of Nations would betray the heart of humanity.

There were many then who did not believe him,
and who dismissed his impassioned pleas as merely the idealistic preachings
    of a minister's son—a college president—
        who in politics was like a babe in the woods.

But history—the story of our tragic years—has merely shown how right he was.

William Agar, editor of the *Louisville Courier-Journal,*
    gave an illustration of this sort of thing the other evening in a radio talk.

In 1920, a United States senator was asked if he could provide a slogan for the election campaigns.
He suggested the slogan, "Americanism" . . .
    and when he was asked what that meant, he replied:

"Damned if I know, but it means a lot of votes."

That cynical and stupid statement was indicative of a frame of mind,
    an attitude,
        a philosophy of selfishness
            and indifference
                not only to the need of a bleeding world . . .
but also to the sacrifices of the men who manned the guns in the Argonne . . .
    and who swept through the streets of Chateau-Thierry . . .
sincerely believing that by their sufferings,

by their wounds,
by their blood and sweat,
they were going to make the world a better place in which to live.

We must avoid both extremes in our thinking today . . .
We must not regard war as purely a human problem to be considered on the
level of economics,
or sociology.
Nor must we regard it as wholly a question for God,
to be considered on the level of theology.

Both God and man are involved!

To believe otherwise is to violate
on one hand the sovereignty of God
and on the other hand the freewill of man.

If God is sovereign and still retains control of the world He has made,
why does He permit war?
This is an old question . . . it is one with which our forefathers wrestled.

Think ye not that the martyrs asked it, as driven with whips they walked up
dungeon steps into the arenas to be torn to pieces by the lions?

Did they not wonder in their hearts
as they were fastened to the stakes and the angry flames leaped up?

Think ye not that the wives and children of the Crusaders asked it
as they waved their tearful farewells while husbands and fathers,
brothers and sweethearts rode off to fight the Turk?

Think ye not that the refugees asked it as the Dutch left the canals and the
flowering farms of Holland . . .
and the Hugenots left the low countries and the fair land of France . . .
and the Pilgrim fathers braved uncharted seas . . .
and the Covenanters stained the purple heather a richer hue?

Think ye not that the question has been asked countless times in every land in every age?

The rolling drum,
    the bugle's call,
        and the beat of marching feet have set the tempo of it in every heart.

The question is as old as pain itself . . .
    as old as human tears,
        as old as suffering and sin.

Let me say at the outset that neither I nor anyone else can dogmatically answer the question. We do not know the mind of God.

We can only submit certain general principles . . .
    we must point out that in the Bible this question is neither raised,
        nor is it considered . . .

Our text from the Epistle of James is the nearest approach we have,
    and here is raised the question of the origin of war . . .

    "From whence comes wars and fightings among you? Come they not
    hence, even of your lusts that war in your members?"

Nowhere in the Bible is the promise given that there will be no war . . .
God never promised a war-less world.

As long as there is sin in the world . . .
    as long as human nature is fallen human nature . . .
        as long as there is greed,
            selfishness,
                and hate in the hearts of men,
                    there will be war.

Let us make no mistake about it . . .
    peace is a product of righteousness

and justice
and love . . .

That is why we must strive to make the world Christian!
There can be no peace while there is hate . . .
there can be no peace while there is envy . . .
there can be no peace while there is injustice . . .

Let us be very clear about that!

Has God ever promised to prevent war in this world
that is still in rebellion against Him?

Why should God prevent war?
We cannot expect blandly to ignore the conditions of God's blessing . . .
go our own way . . .
do as we please . . .
and still enjoy the blessings of peace.

Have we not found that out in our own lives?
We cannot do evil and feel good.
Jesus said very plainly:

> "And ye shall hear of wars and rumors of wars: see that ye be not troubled: for all these things must come to pass, but the end is not yet.

> "For nation shall rise against nation, and kingdom against kingdom: and there shall be famines, and pestilence, and earthquakes, in divers places.

> "All these are the beginning of sorrows."

Why should we expect peace?
What right have we to expect peace?

There is a spiritual law that operates not only in the lives of individuals ...
    but also in the lives of nations ... and the law could be stated thus:

    "Whatsoever a nation soweth, that shall it also reap."

Now, that law is fixed ...
    it is fixed in the economy of God ...
        it is fixed in His eternal justice ...

After all, why do we desire peace?
Let us be as honest as we can.

Some will say what a foolish question ...
    think of the suffering war brings ...
        think of the death and destruction,
            the killing and the murder ...
                the hate and the waste of it all!

Think of men dying at sea in flaming oil ...
    Think of the frantic searchers digging in the ruins of bombed cities
        and lifting out the mangled bodies of old people and children.

Every heart with blood in it will certainly agree with a desire for peace ...
    to put an end to the bloodshed and destruction!

But let me remind you that there is also bloodshed and destruction and waste
in other things and in other directions ... and one hears no national outcry.

What about the ravages and destructions of alcohol that turns men into
beasts,
    that degrades womanhood ...
        that wrecks homes,
            and that ruins health and takes its own toll of human life?
Or what about the mangled bodies at the side of the road?
    What about the waste of human life in our automobile accidents?

What about the waste of human life in this free land by disease
    and slums
        and undernourishment?

Have the humanitarians who are appalled at the results of war felt any
burdens on their hearts as they thought of the Negro people in this
country?

Let us be honest—why do we desire peace?
Is it merely because we shrink from the hardships
    and the suffering that war imposes?

And there *are* hardships,
    and there *are* sufferings—*that,* no one can deny!

Already there are mothers and fathers in this country . . .
    how many we do not know . . .
        who are mourning the death of loved ones in the service of their
country.

Yes, there is suffering
    and there is sorrow . . .
but there may be some whose desire for peace is simply a disguised desire
on their part to lead their own lives uninterrupted without inconvenience
to themselves.

They resent the shortages of this and that . . .
    they resent the rationing of sugar
        and gasoline,
            and perhaps of tea and coffee as well . . .
they do not like the increased taxation
    and the bother and nuisance of black-out preparations . . .
it is all so inconvenient,
    and they long for peace again
        when they will be free to live their own lives in their own way.

I dare to ask the question: what right have we to expect peace?

What did we do with peace when we had it?
     How did we use the twenty-one years of peace after the first World War?

Will you please go back in your memory to the "roaring twenties" and the "tragic thirties"?
May I remind you that the decade that began with 1920
     saw a wave of lawlessness and crime,
          of license and indulgence sweep over this country
               such as it had never seen before . . .
                    and God grant may never see again?

How did we use the peace when we had it?

Have we ever pondered the real value and function of peace?

We are told in Acts 9:31, that after terrific persecution had come upon the Church,
     there was a period of peace in which the churches were edified,
          the Christians walked in the fear of the Lord,
               and in the comfort of the Holy Ghost,
                    and they were multiplied.

The Church then used the period of peace to build up believers in the faith . . .
     to seek the cultivation of the soul.
They used the opportunity to the fullest,
     to live a godly and a holy life . . .
          and they were built-up in the faith.

That suggests to us how peace should be used . . .
for as our Shorter Catechism teaches us,
     "The chief end of man is to glorify God and to enjoy Him forever."

Is that why we desire peace?

What if war has come because we were not fit for peace?
> Had you thought of that?
>> How do you like *that* suggestion?

That God does permit war is a fact . . . and, as I said before,
> we cannot categorically answer why.
But let me suggest one or two reasons.

It may be in order to teach us that war is punishment for sin.
We are appalled by the starvation of the body that war and blockade
imposes upon civilians . . .
> we are shocked by the wounds that the weapons of war inflict.

But the Bible teaches us that the soul is more important than the body . . .
> that human personality is sacred . . .
>> that it is in being a soul that man is in the image of God . . .
>>> and that the greater crime is injury to the soul.
Christ once said a most striking thing . . .

> "Fear not them which, after they have killed the body, have
> nothing more that they can do."

In other words, suppose the body is killed—that is not the all-important thing.
What is all-important is what has happened to the soul!

But what regard have we in America had for the souls of men . . .
What soul-nourishment does our school system provide?
What soul-exercise does the average modern home provide?

The emphasis is not on how long you live . . . but how well!
The measure of a life, after all, is not its duration,
> but its donation!
The important thing is not the quantity of life measured by years,
> but the quality of life measured by goodness!
God's concern is not *how long* we live . . . but *how* we live.

His anxiety for human life is not that it be saved . . .
      but that it be lived in right relationship with Him.

Sin always leads to suffering and misery and shame,
      but we are not inclined to become alarmed about it
            until it breaks out on a large scale.

For example, we as a congregation are not concerned
      over the illness of the Jones family
            in some alley dwelling in a Washington slum . . .

But, if the illness were some infectious disease
that spread until an epidemic laid its yellow clammy hand on our city's life . . .
      then we would become alarmed.

There are other problems in our world
      which are just as contrary to God's love . . .
            His justice
            and His holiness.
Why do we not expect Him to stop them also?

For instance, why does not God stop drunkenness?
                              and crime,
                        and gambling,
                  and prostitution,
                  and slums,
                        and racial injustice,
                              and corruption in politics,
                        and bribery?

Suggestions have been made from time to time that
      action should be taken to prevent these evils . . .
            such as prohibition of alcoholic beverages . . .
                  refusal to legalize betting at race tracks . . .
                        federal proceedings against certain political practices.

But such suggestions bring forth a chorus of protests and shouts of
"personal freedom,"
    "liberty of conscience"
       "rights of the individual" . . .
         and so forth.

The moment some action is suggested to curb other evils,
there is resentment of the idea that there should be any interference
    either by God or man.
Why, then, if personal freedom is so precious a thing,
    should God violate it to interfere with man's war-making?

Yes . . . God permits war as punishment of sin.
When will we learn that God is not mocked?
"Whatsoever a nation soweth that shall it also reap."

Secondly, God permits war in order that we might see what sin really is.

War forces us to examine the very foundations of life itself.
In peace we are complacent about sin.
    We laugh it out of court.
Man feels that God is unnecessary in peace-time.
    He can "get along" without God.

So, what man refuses to learn in times of peace,
    God teaches him in times of war.

In time of war we see the stark reality of the operation of the laws by which
God governs His universe.
We need to be reminded that the world is run according to law . . .
and that to suspend the operation of the law of cause and effect, for instance,
    would be to throw the universe into chaos.

God will no more prevent the outbreak of wars
    than He will prevent injury to a person who jumps from a ten-story building.

War will—and must—show the futility utility of "insurance religion,"
   by which a person has steadfastly believed for years
      that if he just says his prayers and goes to church
         and leads a decent life,
he will be protected by God from the calamities that overwhelm other people.

As far as our own personal religion is concerned,
   we must believe that in the end right will surely triumph . . .
      and that even if we were to lose the war,
         God would vindicate His nature . . .
            and bring out of such an unthinkable conclusion
the establishment of spiritual values and the extension of His kingdom.

We must not permit ourselves to identify the success of the Kingdom of
God with the success of the allied nations in this present world conflict.
God will win . . . even if we are defeated.

God may be permitting this war to lead us back to Him.

"There are no atheists in foxholes"—said the sergeant in Bataan . . .
and men unaccustomed to prayer have tried it while tossing in a rubber boat
on the broad expanses of the ocean.

Not only the men in action on the far-flung battle fronts of this war . . .
   not only the brave seamen who go down to the dangerous seas in ships . . .
      but also their fathers and mothers,
         their brothers and sisters at home,
have come to think more of God in recent days,
   and will yet consider even more seriously their lives
      in relation to His divine plan and His will.

Of Israel it was said: "In their trouble and distress they cried unto God."
It is only natural.
   It is human.
      It is the cry of every creature . . .

Blind to His goodness and kindness in times of peace . . .
     when trouble comes, they remember Him.

We are still the same.

"Far-called, our navies melt away
On dune and headland sinks the fire
Lo, all our pomp of yesterday
Is one with Nineveh and Tyre!
Judge of the Nations, spare us yet,
Lest we forget—lest we forget!"[1]

The most vital question that faces us today is not after all,
     "Why does God permit war?" . . .
          but rather,
               "Are we learning the lesson?"

The Greatest Adventure

"The Greatest Adventure"

New York Avenue Presbyterian Church
Washington, D.C.
January 31, 1943

The operator was pounding out the SOS signal.
The gasoline supply was running out, and soon
they all knew the huge Flying Fortress would have
to be set down at sea.

The eight men in the four motored plane were grim,
and each man had his own thoughts.
Until they had taken off on this flight, they were
strangers to each other.

The fortunes of war had brought them together as
passengers and crew of a ship soon to sink beneath
the waters of the Pacific ocean.

From Honolulu they had headed southwest for a small
island outpost - a tiny speck of land in the broad
waters of the earth's greatest ocean.

Overshooting the island because of a tail wind that
was stronger than the forecast,
and also because the navigator's octant had been
jarred during the take-off, thus probably making his
observations inaccurate.....
          they found themselves lost.

Every man peered out of the windows vainly looking
for land.
The cloud shadows raised false hopes while time and
gasoline ran out relentlessly.

Eight men in a land plane, knowing that soon they
would be forced down on the water.
What would you have thought about?

They were an average bunch of men, with average
American backgrounds.
They came from the west and from the east
          From Texas
               California
                    Washington
                         Pennsylvania
                              and Connecticut
The oldest man among them was fifty-two
          and the youngest thirty years *******.
                                   his junior

75

Introduction to

The Greatest Adventure

The story of Captain Eddie Rickenbacker and his men is one of the most amazing tales of World War II. In October 1942 on a flight from Honolulu to Canton Island in the Central Pacific, he and his seven-man crew overshot their destination by more than a hundred miles. Forced to ditch the B-17 bomber in the ocean, they were adrift for twenty-two days in three rafts. The word *adventure* seems to be a tame word to describe their terrible ordeal, for these men were literally facing death. But in the midst of it all, God was there, and they were rescued on November 11, 1942.

And what is the point for us today? Besides being a memorable story, is there a message from Rickenbacker's ordeal for us?

Indeed there is. Though none of us may have to endure circumstances as harrowing as those of Rickenbacker and his men, God wants to become just as real to us as He was to those men floating on the vast Pacific Ocean.

As the crew learned, God does not usually push Himself into our lives. He waits to be invited, though. He will most assuredly answer us when we truly reach out for Him with all our hearts.

The Greatest Adventure

New York Avenue Presbyterian Church

Washington, D.C.

January 31, 1943

Seek ye the LORD while he may be found. Call ye upon him while he is near. Let the wicked forsake his way, and the unrighteous man his thoughts; and let him return unto the LORD, and he will have mercy upon him; and to our God, for he will abundantly pardon."

—ISAIAH 55:6–7

The operator was pounding out the SOS signal. The gasoline supply was running out, and soon they all knew the huge *Flying Fortress* would have to be set down in the ocean.

The eight men in the four-motored bomber were grim,
    and each man had his own thoughts.
Until they had taken off on this flight, they were strangers to each other.

The fortunes of war had brought them together as passengers and crew of a plane soon to sink beneath the waters of the Pacific Ocean.

From Honolulu they had headed southwest for a small island outpost—
    a tiny speck of land in the broad waters of the earth's greatest ocean.

Overshooting the island because of a tail wind that was stronger than the
forecast,
    and also because the navigator's octant had been jarred during the
takeoff,
        thus probably making his observations inaccurate . . .
            they found themselves lost.

Every man peered out of the windows vainly looking for land.
    The cloud shadows raised false hopes
        while time and gasoline ran out relentlessly.

Eight men in a land-based plane,
    knowing that soon they would be forced down on the water.

What would you have thought about?

They were an average bunch of men, with average American backgrounds.
They came from the west and from the east
    from Texas,
        California,
            Washington,
                Pennsylvania,
                    and Connecticut.
The oldest man among them was fifty-two,
    and the youngest thirty years his junior.

In civilian life they had been average Americans . . .
                                        not particularly religious . . .
their faith and beliefs were vague things—taken for granted . . .
    never discussed much . . .
        seldom expressed.
For the most part they were inarticulate on the subject of God and prayer
and spiritual life.

Now, sitting grimly silent in the plane, listening for the first dry splutter of
the engines . . .
> knowing that it was only a matter of minutes
>> before they would be forced to come down on the water,
>>> they prepared for the crash landing.

They made ready to throw overboard everything that was movable.
The high priority mail they had been carrying was dumped into the ocean . . .
and then the tool box,
> the cots
>> and the blankets . . .
>>> empty thermos bottles,
>>>> a raincoat,
>>>> the baggage,
>>> a briefcase filled with important papers . . .

For, when the moment comes when nothing is left but life,
> one does not hesitate to discard material possessions,
>> no matter how highly esteemed.

The large bomber glided down . . . down . . .
> and a calm voice called out "fifty feet," . . .
>> and then almost immediately "thirty feet."

It was strangely still in the plane.
The muffled roar of the engines seemed far away.
Then the voice again . . . "twenty feet."

They were coming in at ninety miles an hour with the landing flaps and
wheels up so that there would be nothing to snag in the water.

When the ship hit, their pre-arranged plan was carried out with the discipline of a well-trained crew.

In sixty seconds they had launched the life rafts . . .
　　the flimsy crafts in which they were to spend three weeks
　　　　drifting on the eight-foot swells of the Pacific Ocean.

The story of the twenty-one days is a gripping epic of human fortitude and
courage. It should be read by every American
　　and preserved with the sagas of brave men.

One cannot read it without tears.
It is a moving document
　　whether the one writing is Captain Rickenbacker or Lieutenant
Whittaker.

The mere recital of the events themselves is drama,
　　and any attempt at imagining what they went through must end in
failure.
It is quite beyond any of us—well-fed,
　　　　　　　　over-nourished,
　　　　　　comfortable,
　　　　in armchairs by fire-sides—
　　to conceive of that experience.

The sea was a glassy calm, while the sun burned fiercely.
Faces,
　　necks,
　　　　hands,
　　　　　　wrists,
　　　　　　　　legs,
　　　　　　　　　　and ankles burned,
　　　　　　　　　　　　blistered,
　　　　　　　　　turned raw,
　　　　　　　and burned again.

Drenched with the salt spray kicked up by the night winds,
　　flesh stung and cracked and dried,

only to be burned again the next day.

They were like living creatures slowly turning on a spit over the furnace of
the sun.

Captain Rickenbacker described it thus:

> "The sea sent back billions of sharp splinters of light; no matter
> where one looked it was painful. A stupor descended upon the
> rafts. Men simply sat or sprawled, heads rolling on the chest,
> mouths half open, gasping."

During the day the sun poured down upon them like molten metal,
and they longed for the coolness of the night.

But the nights were cold, chilling them to the bone
as they sat huddled together,
cramped,
drenched with spray,
their teeth chattering.
Then they craved the sun.

It was the nights that brought them close to fear.
A cold dense mist always rose around them . . .
but the hardest thing about the dark hours was the fact that
they could never stretch out.

Night after night,
day after day,
this torture of aching muscles,
when no comfort could be found.

All around them the dorsal fins of sharks cut the water—
a grisly reminder of the danger of falling overboard.
Eight men—

cramped in three small rafts—
    with four oranges comprising their entire stock of food.
What chance would you have given them of surviving for three weeks?

Now, these men were not particularly religious.
    Only one of them had a New Testament.
        Most of them could not repeat the Lord's Prayer.
           They knew little or nothing about the Bible.
They were absolutely unskilled in getting in touch with God.

As a matter of fact, they hadn't thought much about God before . . .
    for the most part they had been indifferent to spiritual things.

As a group, religion had for them no everyday reality.

One of them confessed that he had been an agnostic,
    or an atheist if you will.
He did not know the Lord's Prayer,
    and had never taken much stock in prayer.

Captain Rickenbacker himself was not a religious man,
    although he had gone to Sunday School.
His creed was the Golden Rule.

You see, for them religion was a vague inarticulate sort of thing at best.
No one could ever have called these eight men religious fanatics.
They were far from it.

One of the sergeants had a New Testament and, seeing him read it,
    his companions thought that they might all profit by his example.

They held morning and evening prayers,
    pulling the three rafts together,
        then each, in turn, would read a passage.

It was apparent that none of them was familiar with the Bible,
  but there was one passage they never failed to read.
    It was this, Matthew 6:31–34:

> "Therefore take no thought, saying, What shall we eat? or, What
> shall we drink? or, Wherewithal shall we be clothed?

> "For after all these things do the Gentiles seek; For your heav-
> enly Father knoweth that ye have need of all these things.

> "But seek ye first the kingdom of God, and his righteousness;
> and all these things shall be added unto you.

> "Take therefore no thought for the morrow: for the morrow
> shall take thought for the things of itself. Sufficient unto the day
> is the evil thereof."

Now, it is not to be supposed that these men suddenly turned pious.
On the contrary,
  some of them were scornful and bitter because their prayers were not
answered quickly,
  but the others kept on praying with deep-felt hope.

There were times when their tempers broke out savagely,
  as one would brush against the raw flesh of his neighbor,
    and irritation and frayed nerves were expressed in lurid profanity.

But they took a plunge in faith.
They had nothing to lose and everything to gain.
They told God about their troubles and they asked for His help.

What happened?

Well, the first thing was that each man became aware of what had been wrong in his life. Frankly and openly they confessed their past sins.
Out there on the trackless waters of the Pacific
    confessions were made which will never be made public.
They learned things about each other that would never have been suspected.

And pledges were made . . . as each man prayed individually.
One man pledged to be a better father and husband if he were spared.
Another promised he would provide for those dependent upon him.

They asked for forgiveness.
    They made resolutions.
        They promised to start over again and do better,
            if God would help them.

Then they waited in faith.

God took them up on it,
    as He always will when people are earnestly seeking Him.

Lieutenant Whittaker put it this way:

> "For me those blazing days represent the greatest adventure a
> man can have—the one in which he finds his God. We met as
> strangers in the watery waste along the Equator . . . I learned to
> pray. I saw prayer answered."

It was on the eighth day,
    about an hour after the reading of the Scripture
        and the promise God makes in the sixth chapter of Matthew.

Rickenbacker was dozing, with his hat pulled down over his eyes.
A gull appeared from nowhere and landed on his hat.

They all held their breath
and watched with insane and hungry looks
while Rickenbacker reached up his hand,
gradually . . .
slowly.

He rubbed his chin.
He stroked his nose.
He smoothed an eyebrow.

Then with a swift clutch he made the bird prisoner!

The body was carved up and the intestines were used for bait.
One hook was hardly wet before a small mackerel hit it and was jerked into
the raft.
The other line met with the same miraculous result—this time a small sea bass.

This supply of food in the space of a few minutes gave them all fresh hope
and courage.

On the 13th day a squall blotted out the sun,
and their hopes rose that it might bring rain.
They prayed for the squall to reach them,
that their parched throats might be moistened
and that they might be able to catch some water.

But the squall passed them by.

For the first time, Whittaker, the agnostic, now prayed with his whole heart:

"God, you know what that water means to us. The wind has
blown it away. It is in your power, God, to send it back again. It's
nothing to you, but it means life to us."

Some of the others had given up.
Someone said the wind would blow in the same direction for another forty
years.
But the former unbeliever continued his prayer:

> "God, the wind is yours. You own it. Order it to blow back that
> rain to us who need it."

There are some things that may not be explained by natural law.
The wind did not change,
    but the receding curtain of rain stopped where it was.
Then,
      ever so slowly,
          it began moving back toward the rafts—
             against the wind!

The rain squall moved with majestic deliberation.
It was as though a great and omnipotent hand moved it back across the
waves.

They caught a great store of water,
    which brought relief to the baked and burned men.
God provided strength so that three of the men were saved when they had
reached the point of exhaustion.

Lieutenant Whittaker and his two companions had sighted land—an island
fringed with palm trees.

Hour after hour he paddled the cumbersome raft toward the shore and,
    when only about a city block from land,
        the raft was caught in a current that carried them out to sea again.

Whittaker cried out to God in anguish.
Exhausted,
    with his two companions spent,

and with no strength left,
    he made his final prayer:
        "God, don't quit me now!"

He testifies that in the final burst to make the reef,
    the aluminum oars were bent with the power of the stroke,
        but it was not his own power.

He did not have the strength left to bend the oar—he could not have bent a
pin.

He was not conscious of exerting any strength.
It was more as though the oars were working automatically,
    and his hands were merely following their motion.

There were other hands than his on the oars.
Thoroughly exhausted,
    and with three weeks of thirst and hunger behind him,
        Whittaker recognized this as the second miracle.

When they finally reached land,
    they stopped and gave thanks to God for their deliverance.

When Rickenbacker and Bartek were rescued, the Captain said to the
young man:
    "Better thank God for your Bible, son.
    You see now what faith can do for you."

Rickenbacker had been called "lucky."
He was said to bear a charmed life.
    He believed in his "luck."

He had carried for twenty-five years a small crucifix,
    but to him it was more a charm—a good-luck piece—than a religious
symbol.

But ask Rickenbacker now if his rescue was simply a matter of luck.

Whittaker was an atheist once.
Ask him now if there's a God—and if he believes in Him.

These eight men met God out on the broad waters of the Pacific Ocean—
    what happened to them—
        apart from their miraculous rescue?

Whittaker testifies that the whole course of his life has been changed.
He is a new man.
He acknowledges that for forty-one years he had lived a selfish life,
    believing in himself and no one else.
Four months before, he had been quarrelsome and loved an argument.
He saw little good in anyone—
    he was cynical and bitter—
        a hard man.

Notice the change.
Whittaker now says that he accepts everyone as being decent and good until
he proves otherwise.
He is willing to give others the benefit of the doubt,
    and to attribute to them the best of motives.

When he came home,
    he made up with a brother to whom he hadn't spoken in fifteen years . . .

Johnny Bartek has announced his intention to enter the ministry after the
war.

Each man has been changed.
Their dramatic experience has given them a new outlook on life.
Whether the change is a permanent one,
                        time alone will tell.

Now that they are home, it is up to them.
They can, if they wish,
    continue the same fellowship with God that they enjoyed on their rafts . . .
        that supported them and finally rescued them from a horrible death.

I am wondering if it will take starvation,
                         thirst,
                shipwreck,
            bombs,
    and death to make us at home seek God?

These brave men—
    average Americans—
        tried prayer only when every other human resource had failed.
                There was nothing left.

Must we get into such a desperate plight before we avail ourselves of the
power of God?

You and I can follow the same path that these men took.
Only, we can do it in the privacy of our own rooms tonight
    or tomorrow morning,
        rather than on the trackless Pacific.

You can find Him as real and as powerful in your armchair
    or, on your knees in your bedroom . . .
        if you will.

We, too, can take the plunge in faith.
We, too, can take to God our troubles,
                        our problems,
                            our sorrows,
                                our needs.

We, too, will first feel a sense of our unworthiness.
Because, as soon as we begin to pray like that,
the Holy Spirit of God makes us feel our sin . . .
   not only the sin we were willing to confess,
      but also the sin we tried to hide.

It will all come out . . . out into the light of God's presence . . .
   and we'll confess . . .
      and while confessing . . .
         cry out for forgiveness.

After we have confessed our sins, God may tell us things *to do*.

There may be things . . .
   there probably *are* things in our lives that should be set right.
Some things cannot be rectified . . .
   but many things can be—
      and must be—set right,
         before we'll have any peace.

There are two main conditions for fellowship with Christ:

First, we must take time each day to speak to the Lord . . .
   a quiet time that we reserve for Him alone.

In this prayer time . . .
   whether it be in the morning or at night . . .
      whether it be alone or as a family group . . .
we can be specific . . .
   and bring to the Lord whatever problems face us that day—
      whatever matters we have on our hearts.
We can seek His guidance and His strength . . .
   and ask Him to make known to us His will . . .
      just what He wants us to do.

All this is necessary,
  because our God is a shy God in a sense.
He will not come to your heart without your invitation.
  He does not invade your heart's domain.
    He will not break down the door.

He has given to us free wills . . .
  He has dared to make us free agents.

We are the hosts of our hearts . . .
and our heart's door is curiously made . . .
  different from any other door we have ever known.

The latch is on the inside.

The door opens outward,
  and once we have opened it and invited God to come in . . .
    the door does not stay invitingly open.

Slowly it closes of itself.
That is why we must open it again and again—each day we live.

Then, in the second place,
  we must do what God directs us to do.

We must obey His guiding.
The impulses with which He gently tugs at our heartstrings . . .
  the whispers of love and kindness,
    of generosity and benevolence,
      that he sends running down the corridors of our wills . . .
        must be obeyed.

For, if these impulses and whispers are ignored . . .
  then after so long . . .

the messengers, weeping . . .
    go back where they came from,
        and we are left alone again.

The adventure which Captain Rickenbacker shared . . .
    with the six surviving members of the company that floated for three
weeks . . .
    in three small rafts on the Pacific . . .
        has made a profound impression on the thinking of Americans.

There have been other instances, too, where men have found God,
    and found in prayer the avenue that led to God,
        and His divine help,
            without which they would surely have perished.

But we, in this church this morning,
    can have experiences of God just as thrilling.

We are not yet driven to have them as they were.
But we may be . . .
    unless we are willing to seek God while there is yet time.

> "Seek ye the LORD while he may be found. Call ye upon him
> while he is near. Let the wicked forsake his way, and the unright-
> eous man his thoughts; and let him return unto the LORD, and he
> will have mercy upon him; and to our God, for he will abun-
> dantly pardon."[1]

God wants to enter your heart today . . .

    but the latch is on the inside.

        Will you open the door?

A Text from Lincoln

"A Text From Lincoln"

New York Avenue Presbyterian Church

Washington, D.C.

February 14, 1943

The history of the world has largely been the biography of her great men.

There was a time in our own history when youth was inspired by Hero-Worship, when it was definitely a part of our national consciousness and thinking.

Lives of Washington were published in country towns and exchanged by travelling peddlars for anything the farmers had to sell.

Those were the days when a picture of Washington or Lincoln adorned every school room wall, when, on special days, small boys, wriggling uncomfortably in their store-bought suits, pointed to the American flag and recited Washington's Farewell Speech or Lincoln's Gettysburg Address.

And, in the dim sanctuaries of every parlor, along with the pondrous Family Bible on the Victorian table and the hymn books on the old fashioned square piano, there looked down from the walls the likenesses of our venerated national heroes -- Washington
                              Jefferson
                         Lincoln
                    Jackson
               or Lee.

During long winter evenings, the stories of their lives were read aloud to the family, while the flickering firelight made grotesque shadows on the walls, and the tales of their hardships and triumphs became the pattern for every American boy.

Those were the days of great beliefs ---
          belief in the Bible
       belief in prayer
    belief in marriage and the family as permanent
                 institutions
belief in the integrity and worth of America's great men.

Then there dawned the day when the pictures of Washington or Lincoln looked strangely out of place beside the first manifestations of Surrealism....

INTRODUCTION TO

A Text from Lincoln

"This is a time for greatness,
  greatness of soul,
    greatness of faith,
      greatness of thinking,
        greatness of action."

So preached my father in 1943, in the middle of World War II. The "time for greatness" phrase came from Herbert Agar's book, *A Time for Greatness,* which probably inspired this sermon.

Abraham Lincoln also prominently appears in this sermon, not only because my father was fond of quoting him, but also because of Lincoln's connection with the church pastored by my father. New York Avenue Presbyterian Church had been Abraham Lincoln's family church. The Lincoln family pew, which in his day was also the pastor's pew, sits among the other pews in the church sanctuary to this day.

Though our sixteenth President was a regular attender at Sunday worship, and often listened to the Wednesday night prayer meetings from a room adjacent to the sanctuary, he had never joined a church. But the evidence is strong that the pastor, Dr. Phineas D. Gurley, was planning to welcome Lincoln into the membership of New York Avenue Presbyterian Church two days after he was assassinated. It would have been Easter Sunday, 1865.

I included this particular sermon in this volume, not because of Lincoln's connection with my father's church, but because America is once again at war. In recent decades our society has distinctly lacked strong moral and spiritual leadership, both in church and state. In this time of crisis, America must rediscover its moral and spiritual roots.

A search through our history for moral and spiritual leadership will always turn up the name of Abraham Lincoln, the humble man who guided the Union through one of our nation's most tumultuous crises. Now, more than ever, our nation cries for leaders of such rock-hard courage.

Our time is also a time for greatness.

A Text from Lincoln

New York Avenue Presbyterian Church

Washington, D.C.

February 14, 1943

The history of the world has always been the biography of her great men.

There was a time in these United States when youth was inspired by hero-worship,
    when it was definitely a part of our national consciousness and thinking.

Lives of Washington were published in country towns
    and exchanged by traveling peddlers for anything the farmers had to sell.

Those were the days when a picture of Washington or Lincoln adorned every school room wall . . .
    when, on special days,
        small boys, wriggling uncomfortably in their store-bought suits,
            pointed to the American flag,
and recited Washington's Farewell Speech or Lincoln's Gettysburg Address.

And in the dim sanctuaries of every parlor,
    along with the ponderous family Bible on the Victorian table,
        and the hymn books on the old fashioned square piano,

there looked down from the walls the likenesses of our venerated national
heroes—Washington,
    Jefferson,
        Lincoln,
            Jackson,
                or Lee.

During the long winter evenings,
    the stories of their lives were read aloud to the family,
        while the flickering firelight made grotesque shadows on the walls,
            and the tales of their hardships and triumph
                became the pattern for every American boy.

Those were the days of great beliefs—
                        belief in the Bible,
               belief in prayer,
        belief in marriage and the family as permanent institutions,
belief in the integrity and worth of America's great men.

Then, there dawned the day
    when the pictures of Washington or Lincoln looked strangely out of
place
        beside the first manifestations of Surrealism,
and the old family Bible didn't seem to go with modernistic furniture . . .
                              radios . . .
                    and cocktail cabinets.

So, they were relegated together to the Attic of Forgotten Things . . .
    and there went with them
        some of the most stabilizing influences in American life.

Along with our higher education came a sort of national debunking
contest.
It suddenly became smarter to revile than to revere—
    more fashionable to depreciate than to appreciate.

In our classrooms we no longer worshiped great men,
  we merely took their dimensions and ferreted out their faults.

We decided that it was silly to say God sent them for any special task.
They couldn't help being what they were . . .
  they were merely the "creatures of their time" . . .
    the products of their environments.

We failed to realize that when we were denying the existence of great men,
  we were also denying the desirability of great men.

The result was that a generation began to grow up
  without the guiding star of hero-worship . . .
    holding in their hands no keys of certainty
      with which to open the doors of knowledge and life . . .
        only a bunch of rather pitiful, bedraggled question marks.

We had become a more sophisticated people,
  somewhat cynical of the cherished beliefs of our ancestors . . .
    a little hard-boiled . . .
      rather blasé . . .
        frankly skeptical of old fashioned sentimentalities.

Nevertheless, we were shocked on the evening of Armistice Day last November to hear Lieutenant General Lesley J. McNair
  speak for the Army's high command to the boys of our country in the service.

He made a plea to American troops to make themselves into fighting devils.

"We must hate," said the General, "with every fiber of our being.
We must lust for battle;
  our object in life must be to kill;
    we must scheme and plan night and day to kill."
Now, these words shocked us.

We recognize that our Army must be made into an efficient fighting machine,
    but we recoil from the statement:
        "We must hate with every fiber of our being."

Any effort to whip up hate in cold blood will not work—it must not work!

In the name of God,
                    we must not hate.
In the name of Him whose first words from the cross were a prayer for the forgiveness of His enemies,
                    we must not hate.
In the name of humanity,
    and for the sake of our own souls,
        we must not hate.

As a matter of fact, the people most affected by war do not hate.
You might expect the people of Coventry
                    or London
                        or the Clydeside . . .
whose homes were blasted,
    whose families were wiped out,
        to hate fiercely.

Yet such is not the case.

Dr. John Bonnell, of the Fifth Avenue Presbyterian Church of New York City,
    told the ministers of Washington a few weeks ago that
        during his recent visit to Great Britain
            in which he saw destruction beyond his imagining—
on every hand the results of the furious German air attacks
                on England and Scotland . . .

he found not a single trace of hate anywhere.
The British people, he declared, do not hate the Germans.
There were no smouldering fires of hate . . .

only a grim, quiet determination not to give in,
    to share with each other,
      to stand together,
to make every sacrifice to ensure that this thing would not happen again.

As they dig in the ruins of their homes
    and tenderly lift out the mangled bodies of little children,
      they dream of a new world in which all children,
        German as well as British,
          will be safe.

You might expect again that our men, as they go into action,
    highly trained,
      ready for combat,
        are consumed with hate.
Yet such is not the case.

I have not yet heard a single soldier or sailor express any hatred of the enemy.

It is with sore hearts that our boys are fighting today.
Their hearts ache at the suffering war imposes.
Often with tears in their eyes do they man their guns,
    and it is a grim and serious mood in which our air forces drop their bombs.

There is no blood lust,
    no fierce hate—
      only the realization that the enemy must be defeated
        for the sake of all mankind,
         and the new world they hope to make possible.

The enemy's doctrines they detest.
They hate what he has done . . .
    but after all . . .
      they know that the enemy soldier is a victim of a wicked philosophy.

He laughs and he cries.

 He gets wet and tired and homesick just as they do.

He loves *his* wife and children,

 and somewhere people are praying for *his* safety.

Our men are not going to hate the other men against whom they fight.

It is enough that we hate all that they represent.

After he became President, Lincoln made only three notable addresses—the
First Inaugural,

 the Gettysburg Address,

  and the Second Inaugural.

The *London Times* called the Second Inaugural the most sublime state paper
of the century.

I think all will agree that its grandest passage is the last paragraph:

> "With malice toward none, with charity for all, with firmness in
> the right as God gives us to see the right, let us strive on to finish
> the work we are in, to bind up the nation's wounds, to care for
> him who shall have borne the battle and for his widow and his
> orphan, to do all which may achieve and cherish a just and
> lasting peace among ourselves and with all nations."

Here is a text for today.

When we contrast it with the statement of General McNair,

 we will see at once the greatness of Lincoln on the one hand,

  and the absence of moral conviction of our time on the other.

Dr. Phineas Gurley, the pastor of this church, who was Lincoln's friend and
minister during the four years Lincoln was in the White House,

 preached the funeral sermon in the East Room of the White House.

Dr. Gurley said:

"I speak what I know and testify, what I have often heard him say, when I affirm that God's guidance and mercy were the props on which Abraham Lincoln humbly and habitually leaned, that they were the best hope he had for himself and for his country.

"This it seems to me, after being near him steadily, and with him often for more than four years, is the principle by which, more than by any other, he, being dead, yet speaketh.

"Yes, by his steady, enduring confidence in God, and in the complete ultimate success of the cause of God, which is the cause of humanity, more than in any other way, does he now speak to us, and to the nation he loved and served so well.

"By this he speaks to his successor in office,
   and charges him to have faith in God.

"By this he speaks to the members of his cabinet, the men with whom he counseled so often, and associated with so long,
   and he charges them to have faith in God.

"By this he speaks to all who occupy positions of influence and authority in these sad and troublous times,
   and he charges them all to have faith in God.

"By this he speaks to this great people, as they sit in sackcloth today, and weep for him with a bitter wailing, and refuse to be comforted,
   and he charges them to have faith in God;

"and by this he will speak through the ages, and to all rulers and peoples in every land, and his message to them will be: Cling to liberty and right, battle for them, bleed for them, die for them if need be,
   and have confidence in God."

Surely Dr. Gurley was right.
  Abraham Lincoln is speaking to the ages.
He is speaking to us now,
    and he is saying to this generation,
        "Have faith in God."

I believe that is one message of which we are sorely in need.

America needs a faith today that will match its crisis. It needs the faith of the founding fathers and mothers. It needs the old fashioned faith in God that supported and strengthened our American pioneers during their times of peril and distress.

Our fathers and mothers were not ashamed of their faith.
They believed in God.
They were not ashamed to pray.
To them faith was as real as fire,
    and prayer was as real as potatoes.
And their faith gave them certainty of conviction,
    a comforting assurance within,
        and an invincible courage that brought victory.

God honored them because they honored Him.

What was the stuff that old fashioned religion was made of?
It was made of great beliefs.
It cast its anchor deeper than guesses,
                    or notions,
                        or fancies.
It was not a walking question mark . . .
                it was a standing conviction.

Storms could not shake it . . .
                floods could not wash it away.
It was the great beliefs of Washington,
                    Franklin,

Jefferson
and Lincoln that made them great.
They accepted the universe and they accepted God.

Democracy,
which reaches its highest peak in this country,
will fail when God is forgotten and His Book neglected.

The strongest bulwark of our American heritage is the Christian home.
When that goes—
our American heritage goes with it.
Let us make no mistake about that.

There was a prophetic quality in the things that Lincoln said,
and he spoke for the future more truly than he knew.

He was not aware of the import of his words,
else he would never have said as he did in his Gettysburg Address,
"The world will little note nor long remember what we say here."

Lincoln might indeed have been speaking of this present situation when he
said,

> "Fellow citizens, we cannot escape history . . . No personal
> significance or insignificance can spare one or another of us. The
> fiery trial through which we pass will light us down, in honor
> and dishonor, to the latest generation . . . We shall nobly save or
> meanly lose the last, best hope of earth.

> "The real issue . . . is the eternal struggle between these two prin-
> ciples—right and wrong—throughout the world. It is the same
> spirit that says, 'You toil and work and earn bread, and I'll eat it.'
> No matter in what shape it comes, whether from the mouth of a
> king who seeks to bestride the people of his own nation and live
> by the fruit of their labor, or from one race of men as an apology
> for enslaving another race, it is the same tyrannical principle."

This is a time for greatness—
    greatness of soul,
        greatness of faith,
            greatness of thinking,
                greatness of action.

As Herbert Agar has so well expressed it in his book *A Time for Greatness,*

> "Here are eternal opposites. The United States has become the shield and symbol of freedom, as Germany is the shield and symbol of piracy," of the doctrine that the strong must conquer and enslave the weak.

> "We have not yet deserved the responsibilities which are ours; but we have inherited them. If we try to deny them we shall lose our souls.

> "One awkward truth about our position is that Germany and Japan, standing for simple piracy, can establish their world upon the field of battle. We cannot. Victory in the field is everything for them; they have attained their end when they have spilled sufficient blood. Victory in the field is barely a beginning for us. It is essential, yet it is nothing in itself. It can only be made to bear fruit if we can lift ourselves to the practice of those 'humdrum decencies . . . in millions of undistinguished lives' and 'elementary rightness of action.' Here is the heaviest part of America's duty. It cannot be met on the production lines of our great factories, or with the inventive genius of our engineers. It can only be met in the quality of our daily lives."[1]

In the words of Professor George Fox,

> "Let's not fight for money.
> Let's not fight for markets.
> Let's not fight for a higher standard of living.

Let's fight for an idea . . .
We can say, 'We too are strong, but we will use our strength, not
to take away from the weak, but to defend the weak.

" We do not like strength for its own sake.
Strength for its own sake is ugly and brutal and blind.
We exert our strength to defend the only things that make life
tolerable: honor and beauty and truth and loving kindness . . .

"Let's fight for the independence of the South American
Republics, not because if we do they will trade with us, but
because if we do they will have the right to trade freely, without
compulsion, with whomsoever they wish.

"Let's do it even if we lose money.
"Let's do it because that is the kind of world we think men
should live in.

"Are we ashamed to be as good as this?
Are we afraid of being called idealists?

"If so, we have already given away America . . .

"Everything is unknown about the future save this alone: if the
American idea prevails, the future will offer man some dignity and
some chance for self-improvement. If the American idea is presently
extinguished, the future will be dark for uncountable years.

"And the American idea cannot be saved by the sword alone; it
can only exist only if we live it.
The occasion is piled high with difficulty, and we must rise with
the occasion . . . Fellow-citizens, we cannot escape history."

The Armor of God

An Address to
the St. Andrews Society of Washington, D.C.
at their annual
"Kirkin' o' the Tartan" Service
Sunday Evening, May 2, 1943

Introduction to

The Armor of God

At some point during World War II, the Washington, D.C., chapter of the St. Andrews Society, a networking organization for Scots with chapters all over the world, came to my father and asked him to create a religious service for them. The result was the "Kirkin' o' the Tartan" service, which has become an annual event for St. Andrew's Society chapters everywhere.

This message was chosen for inclusion in this volume because its sentiments desperately need to be heard throughout America today: "We have taken far too much for granted. We have assumed far too glibly that this is a Christian nation."

And these words ring out from 1943, which became chillingly true after September 11, 2001: "We may as well accept the fact that God is not going to defeat falling bombs, nor is He going to arrest the speeding course of bullets in any magic sort of protection."

America has yet to understand that we must fulfill the conditions for God's blessings before we can expect to receive them. Simply singing "God Bless America" over and over is not going to do the job.

The Armor of God

An Address to
the St. Andrews Society of Washington, D.C.
at their annual
"Kirkin' o' the Tartan" Service

Sunday Evening, May 2, 1943

Take up the whole armor of God, that ye may be able to withstand in the evil day, and having done all, to stand.

—EPHESIANS 6:13, ASV

To heath and moor and silent glen
The Scottish spring has come again.
The hills above Innellan wear
Brown heather now, and everywhere
The throstle and the blackbird pour
Their song out as they did before.
The rowan tree has come to bud
And every foamy burn's at flood;
Wild hyacinth and blue-bell grow
Under the larches where, the slow
Mist hovers over the mountain-side,
The coast of Arran and the Clyde,
But silent glen and moor and hill
Are Britain—and unconquered still."[1]

"Unconquered still."

115

Yes, by the grace of God,
                           unconquered still.

There was a time when it looked as if,
    for the first time since 1066,
        the foot of the invader would walk upon the soil of Britain.

In the summer of 1940,
                     it looked black indeed,
and then there rose up on heroic wings
    the valiant young men of whom Mr. Churchill said:

"Never in the field of human conflict was so much owed by so many to so
few."

The defense of Britain by the R. A. F. will rank among the brightest epics of
human courage and devotion to duty.

To the side of the people of Britain
    came thousands upon thousands of the men of Canada,
        responding as they have always done,
                        generously,
                          bravely,
                          and with enthusiasm.

From each of the nations making up the British Commonwealth came help
in men and munitions of war.
Australia and New Zealand responded,
                     as did India and South Africa.
The Fighting French,
    the Dutch,
        the Belgians,
            the Poles,
                the Norwegians,

the Czechs,
the Greeks
carried on the struggle at the time when the skies were darkest,
and only the indomitable spirit of free people could carry on.

All the while,
these allied nations had the moral support
and the enormous material assistance of this great Republic,
which sent over supplies without stint or measure.

The immediate cause of Britain's entry into the war was an attack made
upon Poland,
in direct breach of a pledge deliberately offered by those who afterwards
broke it.
This was only the last of a whole series of broken promises, as the world will
testify.

The immediate cause of America's entry into the war was the treacherous
attack on Pearl Harbor,
even while Japan's emissaries were still conferring with our State
Department
and talking peace.

Treachery and broken pledges,
trickery and lies,
promise and betrayal,
these were the torches that set our world on fire.

With this method of the broken promise
goes contempt for the rights of the weak and the small.
In such a world there can be no justice and no freedom.

It must be confessed that neither the British nor the Americans have at all
times served justice and freedom and truth as we should.

There is much in the history of this Republic and in the history of Britain
of which we ought to be ashamed.

The American treatment of the Indians is not an honorable story . . .
   nor is the relationship between the white and the colored peoples of
America as it should be.

In her conquest of empire,
   Britain has not always followed justice,
      nor cared much about the freedom of others.

Both nations are sinners.

But, in our common heritage we have believed in these things,
   and honored them,
      so that an appeal to them is never without effect among us.
When the issues have been clear we have always ranged ourselves on their
side.

If the blood,
   the sweat,
      the toil,
         and the tears of this present struggle are not to be in vain,
we must dedicate ourselves more deeply to them than in the past,
   and serve them in the years to come with greater consistency.

We know perfectly well what life would be under the Nazis.
Freedom is abolished in practice and repudiated in theory.
   Truth is suppressed and replaced by propaganda.
      Lying has become a science,
                     and cruelty an art.
In Germany,
   justice is explicitly declared to be such treatment of each individual
as may best serve the interest of the State;
   and that is a sheer denial of all that we mean by justice.

Against this idolatry of the State
   we must proclaim that only to God is absolute loyalty due.
And God is the Father of all men,
   so that His children have their value and worth
      independently of any earthly allegiance,
         and all alike are entitled to fair dealing.

What we have learned to understand by justice
            is rooted and grounded in the sovereignty of God.

To love God is necessarily to love one's country . . .
   but to love one's country is not necessarily to love God.

Since God's purposes are never defeated,
   it follows that to the extent that our purposes are identical with His
      we can never lose.

Our enemies have an intrinsically wicked philosophy of life—
   it is anti-human,
      anti-God,
         anti-Christian.

But, we are fighting to keep open the possibility
      of a civilization governed by Christian principles;
we are fighting—
   not so much to defend a Christian civilization,
      as to make one possible.

If this is God's cause,
         as we believe it to be,
                  He will not let it fail.

God's law,
   God's truth,
      and God's purpose will win,

whether we win or lose.

We dare not identify the cause of the United Nations with the Kingdom of God.

However, if we remain with God,
                if we are on His side,
                        then victory will be ours...
though at any one moment it may look like defeat,
                        feel like defeat,
                and smell like defeat.

The Cross looked like defeat too,
    but it was the condition of Christ's greatest victory.

By what course God will bring His cause to victory, we cannot know . . .
    we dare not suppose that if our cause is God's cause
        it will triumph quickly or without loss.

We must realize that behind the force of the Nazi armies
    lies the still more formidable fact of Nazi fanaticism.
There you have a generation of young men and women trained for war.

For eight years or more they have been living in a mental concentration
camp.
They have seen nothing,
    heard nothing,
        and learned nothing except what their teachers wished.
Their minds have been sealed.
They are ready at the bidding of a single man to give themselves for a cause.

We know that cause to be desperately wicked and evil,
but they have been trained to believe that it has the highest claim on their
devotion.

To defeat them, therefore,
    we must see to it that our faith burns as fiercely as theirs.

The initial success of the totalitarian armies
    lay not only in their military equipment,
        but chiefly because they used it with a religious enthusiasm—
not with the fire of a true faith—
                    but with the fire of a false one.

We can match the enemy in arms.
We have now reached the place where our equipment is superior to theirs.
We have and we will continue to match them in courage,
    for we have only to think of Narvik
        and Dunkirk
          and Dieppe,
            of Greece
              and Crete
            and El Alamein,
        of Bataan
      and Corregidor
    and Guadalcanal
to be sure that our courage is as great as theirs.
We have only to think of the men of the *Boise*
                  and the *Yorktown*
            and Torpedo Squadron 8,
        the men of the *Campbell*
      and of the *Rawlpindi*
to feel a deep pride in the heroism of men
    who by their devotion to duty make us all ashamed.

In the words carved on the soldiers' memorial tower on the campus of the
University of Toronto:

    "Take these men for your ensamples.
    Like them remember that prosperity can only be for the free,
    That freedom is the sure possession of those alone who have the
    courage to defend it.

    "Nothing is here for tears, nothing to wail or knock the breast;

no weakness, no contempt, dispraise or blame;
nothing but well and fair, and what may quiet us in a death so
noble."

But, can we match our enemies in faith?
They have a faith in a false God—
    what about our faith in the true and living God?
Can their zeal for anti-Christ be overcome by our indifference to Christ?

Can their devotion to their false absolute be matched
                                        by our emphasis on a false freedom,
which thinks that every appeal for sacrifice
    is a violation of Constitutional rights,
        or property rights,
            of the right to organize
                or to bargain collectively?

We are united so far because we have a common hate—
                                        but where is our common love?

Shall we be united nations only because we hate the same devil—
    or because we love the same God?

This is important.

The most important thing of all is that we put on the whole armor of God.
Victory will be ours only on condition that we seek first the Kingdom of
God
    and turn again to Him in prayer.
We must remember that we are not praying as Americans who happen to be
Christians,
                or as Britons who happen to be Christians,

but it must be as Christians
                who happen to be American or British.

Otherwise, we fall into the error of our enemies,
  whose distinctive sin it is that they put nationality first.

We pray to our Father—the Father of all mankind—
  that He will enable us to preserve for all His family
    the justice,
      the freedom,
        and the love of truth which are threatened now.

We pray that His name may be hallowed in all the world—
  in Russia where men deny it altogether,
    in Germany where they take it in vain . . .
and in our own country where our reverence has been but half-hearted.

Let us not deceive ourselves,
                we have taken far too much for granted.

We have assumed far too glibly that this is a Christian nation.

By what standard can she be adjudged Christian,
  when the majority of her people
    have not even nominal connection with the Christian Church . . .
when so many of her children are brought up as pagans,
  with no religious education,
    no instruction about God . . .

when on any Sunday morning all around us
  families use the Lord's Day for pleasure,
    for lazy indulgence,
      with never a thought of the God Who made them?

Can America be called a Christian nation
  when her people act as if Christ had never lived at all?

Are the policies of our government based upon the teachings and the principles of Christ?

Is it the will of God that motivates the legislators,
    or is it the well organized, well-financed pressure groups?

Do the representatives of the people vote in obedience
    to the still small voice of conscience and of God?

Think, if you will, of the people
    who at this present moment are influencing most strongly
        the lives of the citizens of this great Republic—
            are they Christians?
Are their influences Christian?

If we dare to pray that God's will may be done throughout the world . . .
    and if it is our hope that the travail and the agony,
        the suffering and the death,
            the horror and the cruelty of this war will bring about a better
world—
    then we must become better men and women.

We cannot dedicate ourselves to the doing of so much of God's will as suits
our own convenience . . .
    nor can we come to terms with God . . .
        or try to bargain with Him for the lives of our loved ones
            or the protection of our property.

We may as well accept the fact that God is not going to deflect falling bombs,
    nor is He going to arrest the speeding course of bullets
        in any magic sort of protection.

The preservation of property and insurance from physical wounds
    is nowhere guaranteed in the Scriptures . . .
        and must be no part of our Christian faith.

The repetition of the Lord's Prayer—
    "Our Father, Which art in heaven, hallowed be Thy name,
    Thy will be done on earth as it is in heaven" . . .

certainly imposes upon them that pray it the obligation to do their part.

If the Kingdom of God is to come upon earth,
    then people must live in accordance with God's will.

It must be freely admitted that
    so far the war has not profoundly affected the daily lives of all our people.
Far too many of us are still living as if nothing were happening across the
water.

We read in letters from Britain of our relatives having two eggs per month . . .
    we read of their losing every stick of furniture
        and all their material possessions in an air raid . . .
            but it is all so distant.
We are so far removed from the dust and the explosions and the blood.

Most of us are still living in the same comfortable manner.
We talk a lot about ration books
                 and coupons
             and points . . .
we grumble and complain about the inability to get domestic help . . .
    we fuss about the rising cost of living,
        about prices and black markets . . .
we complain about the crowds
    and how we have to stand in line for almost everything.

And yet, when we are honest, we are bound to admit that
    we get enough sugar,
        enough butter,
            enough meat.

We find restricted use of the car has not upset our lives—
　　merely rearranged them—
　　　　and perhaps for the best.

We talk about our sacrifices to buy war bonds—
　　as if it were a sacrifice—
　　　　as if we were being generous!

We are not giving anything in investing our money in the safest investment—
　　humanly speaking—in the world today.

No, with the exception of the homes that have already known bereavement,
　　with the exception of the men who have come home
　　　　bearing the marks of war—wounded,
　　　　　　having lost their sight
　　　　　　　　or an arm
　　　　　　　　or a leg . . .
with the exception of the people among us who have looked into the
sorrows of war,
　　most of us know nothing about it.

We still have too much time to think of ourselves . . .
　　we are still dedicated to the love of self . . .

Selfishness and greed are still the dominating forces at work in our midst
today,
　　so that a great deal of our talk about our defense of the four freedoms
　　　　is nothing but cant and humbug.
　　　　　　It is sheer hypocrisy.

What most of us mean by freedom is freedom from interference,
　　so that we can go on living in the same easy,
　　　　　　　　　　complacent,
　　　　　　　　　　selfish way.

Not that they would always be surrounded by happiness,
   but that they would be able to find a joy in sorrow.

And He promised them trouble.
He was a realist, this Jesus.
He never blinked at facts,
   and He would not for a moment have any of His followers blink at facts.

He did not promise to rescue His followers *from* trouble,
   but to rescue them *in* trouble.

You see, your theology broke down as it should,
   as it had to,
      because it was not founded on truth or fact.

Your own theology had become a sort of charm—
   a good luck piece—
      a sort of theological rabbit's foot.

As long as your husband was safe . . . it worked . . .
But there was no connection.
It was coincidence.
He was safe...
   but your faith was in *your theology* rather than in your *religion*.

Like the horticulturist who becomes more concerned about his flowerpots
   than about the flowers that grow in them.

In days of old,
   primitive men wore amulets around their necks to ward off evil spirits.
They believed themselves to be surrounded by evil spirits.
They were in the air,
   in the water,
      in the forests,
         on the mountains.

And by wearing charms these primitive men believed themselves safe from
harm.

But we now know that the elements of which our early ancestors were
afraid
    are in fact benevolent . . .
        necessary to our existence and well being.
A wise and kindly God has so arranged the natural forces which sustain our
lives.

Religion is *not a way of getting God on your side*
    so that you can be protected from the world . . .

True religion is a power that enables you to live in harmony with God
    and your fellow men
        in the world *as it is.*

True religion faces the facts of life—
    never blinks at a single one of them.

It is realistic . . .
    because the things it believes are not dependent upon chance happenings . . .
        but are unchanged by whatever happens in the world . . .
            unchanged by the exigencies of peace or of war.

We Americans have an adolescent view of life and of death.
As a nation we have not yet grown up.
We still talk like children,
    and we think like children . . .
        and boast like children:
"Our side always wins . . .
    we have never been licked—
        we can lick the whole world . . .
            we are bigger and stronger than any other nation on the earth."

Now, that is the talk of children on a national scale.
That's how children boast to each other.
We want to win in whatever we do.

In games, we consider the results more important than the game itself.
In war, we want victory—
    but we don't like to pay the price of victory . . .
      we don't like to think about our casualties.

We are still adolescent.
We want to make war fun—
    but war isn't fun.
It never has been fun,
    and it never will be fun.
War is hell—
    unbelievable hell.

In the midst of war,
    we are not yet mentally or emotionally adjusted to war.
We must have our pleasures and our entertainments.

We have no sense of national decency or the fitness of things.

Only a few days ago, 41,000 people jammed a race track
    and bet over three million dollars on the horses,
even when terrible things were happening on the beaches at Tarawa and
Salerno.

There was an almost indecent insistence
    that nothing should interfere with the pleasure of the beaches
      at Miami and Atlantic City.

It is not fair to live in peace time with God,
    managing your own affairs,

thinking you don't need God,
and then *in times of war to blame God for not being real!*

It is childish and almost blasphemous to feel
    that God is responsible for sending such things as war.
We can't blame God for the war.
    He did not make it or cause it.

God is not to be blamed
    because a Japanese torpedo sank the ship on which your husband was
serving.

You can't blame God
    if a burst of anti-aircraft brings down the bomber in which your son is
flying.

And it imposes too great a strain on any theology
    to expect God to throw a protective screen around one individual in a
crew.

Most of our fighting men will come back,
    but it will not mean that God threw around them any special protection . . .
        anymore than it would be true to say that
            He permitted those who will not come back to be killed.

You can't blame God for the casualties any more than you can blame God
    for the screaming tornado
        that ripped a path through Georgia and South Carolina.

You can't think of God as looking down over the balconies of heaven
    and causing a rain-swollen river to overflow its banks
        and wash away people's houses.

What we call the acts of God are so named
    because they were unforseen by the calculations of man . . .
        and because they are beyond the powers of men to prevent or control.

But, they are not deliberate acts of God
   in the sense that He decided at a particular place to do this damage or
that.

"It is true, you see, that *your* theology broke down—*as it should.*

But, that does not mean that God has failed or ceased to exist.
It does not mean that there is nothing to believe in.
You still have grounds for faith and hope.

Placing our lives in the hands of God does not mean that we shall be
coddled
   or protected from the effects of the causes we set in motion.

Your husband did not lose his life—he gave it.
And although you may not see him again in the form you knew and loved . . .
   he will be near you in dear, strange ways . . .
      ways that you will feel and know and understand . . .
         because there is no death for believers . . .
            only eternal life.

He still loves you . . .
   even as you still love him . . .
He still lives in the beauty of eternal life . . .
   and this part of life that is lived in the body is to be measured
      not in its length of years . . .
         but in its intensity of expression.

Many live to be very old . . .
   but have never lived deeply.
Some die young . . .
   but have lived to the full . . .

For us who are Christians, there is this assurance:
   While we live, *Christ is with us;*
      When we die, *"we are with Christ."*

I tell you what is true:
    They live and breathe with you . . .
        and you will feel them close . . .
            in dear, strange ways . . .
                close by your side.
They live!
    they know!
      they see!
They smile with that certain knowledge of the end of all things.
They see the end . . .
    the true victory . . .
      the final peace . . .
They are glad . . .
    and they know now . . .
      that there is no death.

The American Dream

New York Avenue Presbyterian Church

Washington, D.C.

November 19, 1944

In sixty seconds they had launched the life rafts....
the flimsy craft in which they were to spend three
weeks drifting on the eight-foot swells of the
Pacific ocean.

The story of their adventures is a gripping epic
of human fortitude and courage.
It should be read by every American and preserved with
the sagas of bravery.

One cannot read it without tears.
It is a moving document whether the author is Captain
Rickenbacker or Lt. Whittaker.

The mere recital of the events themselves is drama,
and any attempt at imagining what they went through
must end in failure.

It is quite beyond any of us, well-fed
                    over-nourished
                    comfortable
                in arm-chairs by firesides
    to conceive of that experience.

The sea was a glassy calm while the sun burned fiercely.
Faces
    necks
        hands
            wrists
                legs
                and ankles burned
                    blistered
                turned raw and burned again.
Drenched with the spray kicked up by the night winds,
flesh stung and cracked and dried,
    only to be burned again the next day.

They were like living creatures slowly turning on
a spit over the furnace of the sun.

Captain Rickenbacker described it thus:
    "The sea sent back billions of sharp splinters
of light; no matter where one looked it was painful.
A stupor descended upon the rafts. Men simply sat
or sprawled, heads rolling on the chest,
mouths half open, gasping."

INTRODUCTION TO

The American Dream

Ask a modern American what the American Dream means to him and you are likely to get back the answer that for him it means having a good job, and the freedom to do as you please, and to pursue life the way you want.

The tragedy of modern America is that we seem to have lost sight of our centuries-old understanding of the American dream, summed up in this sermon in the words from the Pledge of Allegiance: "One nation, indivisible, with liberty and justice for all."[1]

In this message my father brings a word that every living American needs to hear—that a truly democratic society with just and equal laws is not possible without the strong influence of the Christian faith. Only when we know that there is a Creator God, in whose sight all men are created equal and to whom we are all accountable, will we strive to create a just society.

My hope and prayer is that in our time we will rediscover the compelling power of these principles, so that America will experience a rebirth of the American Dream. Then we will truly become "one nation, under God, with liberty and justice for all."

The American Dream

New York Avenue Presbyterian Church

Washington, D.C.

November 19, 1944

It is said about Columbus's discovery of America
    that he was on a search for spices,
and trying to prove that the Indies might be found by sailing directly west.
Instead he discovered America.

Surely, there was Providence in it—
    God's guiding hand.

The thoughtful American must be impressed by
    the sense of America's mission in the world—
        and find a commanding imperative—
not alone in its origin,
    but also, and supremely,
        in its destiny.

What if Providence were separating a people out of the Old World
    to begin a new experiment . . .
        that through this new beginning . . .
            the Old World itself might begin anew?

Up to this point in history,
    it would seem that America was humanity's latest chance . . .
        perhaps the last chance . . .
although, there are other nations God could use and might use . . .
    if we Americans reject our high destiny.

Two weeks ago, I met on the train a lieutenant in the United States Army,
    who had just returned from fighting in Italy.
He had been in the North African campaign . . .
    he had fought in Sicily . . .
        and he wore the Purple Heart ribbon with his campaign ribbons.

I asked him what he thought of America.
It was a hard question to ask a man who had been gone so long,
    who had been fighting for his country and who had been wounded in
action. He said that after what he had seen in North Africa and in Italy,
    he appreciated America more than ever.
He described the filth and squalor of cities and towns he had seen . . .
    he spoke of Tunis and Bizerte.
He told me of his impression of the Arabs and the natives of North Africa.
He had been deeply impressed with their misery, and their slums.

Learning that he was a resident of Washington,
    I asked him if he had seen Washington's slums—
        some of them within a stone's throw of Capitol Hill.
I asked him if he was familiar with "King's Row,"
    the brothels of Ninth Street,
        the dens of iniquity of which Washington has so many.

I suggested to him that while I had never seen Bizerte,
    I was quite sure that Bizerte had nothing on us.

I asked him some rhetorical questions—
    not expecting answers—
        but rather to make him think,

and to divert his attention from the bottle of rum in his raincoat pocket, which,
      he had told me, he intended to finish between Roanoke and Washington:

"What is America?" I asked.
      "What does America mean to you?"

"Did anyone in North Africa, in Italy, or in Sicily ever ask you that question?"
"And if they had, what would you have said?"

Surely, America means more than "The Arsenal of Democracy". . .
      more than just the generous source of Lend Lease.

In the countries that have been liberated by our fighting men,
      the children crowd around our soldiers and beg for chewing gum and
candy.
These are among the chief interests of our *own* children,
      so, that is natural enough.

But, to the parents of these children in liberated countries,
      America is a place where people have so much to eat
            that they can afford to waste food.

And so, the parents stand at the end of the chow lines
      and carry off in containers,
            in their hands,
                  or wrapped up in their aprons,
                        the food that is so essential to their very lives.

Before the war, America seemed to mean to the rest of the world
      a land of luxury and extravagance:
            spectacular advertising;
                  huge electric and neon signs;
                        streamlined trains;
                              magnificent automobiles;

penthouses and chromium plating;
skyscrapers;
baseball;
Hollywood movies;
and Hollywood morals.

But, we know that the *real* America is not to be found
in the night clubs of New York
or in the movie colony in California . . .
just as we know that America's appreciation of music
is not to be judged by Sinatra;
and just as we know that her conception of government
is not to be measured by Mayor Hague of Jersey City or Gerald L. K.
Smith.

I came to this country as a quota-immigrant,
and in the process of becoming naturalized,
I was required to learn something about this land
which I had chosen of my own free will to be my home.

I had to learn, by comparison with the land of my birth,
the things that make America distinctive,
and in which I share with you, a deep and thankful pride.

I believe I am able to speak on this question:
"What does America mean to the world?"

I know what America meant to me and to my fellow countrymen.
When I left Scotland all alone and set sail for the New World,
I knew from my own experience
what it must have meant to the Pilgrim Fathers . . .
when they watched the headlands of England disappear under the horizon,
and then turned their faces to the West.

They landed on Cape Cod in November, 1620,

and finding the soil unsuitable for agriculture,
    they sailed across Cape Cod Bay,
        and established their settlement at Plymouth.

At first, they thought they would be governed by the charter that had been granted to the Virginia colony,
    but they discovered that its provisions did not extend that far.

There was a dazzling exhilaration in the thought that they were free from all law and authority.
But their Calvinistic training asserted itself.
Their stern piety and wisdom took charge . . .
    and they determined to have authority from within . . .
        if there was to be none from without.

They drew up one of the most significant documents in American history—
    the Mayflower Compact—
        which called for just and equal laws.

This was a new concept, a departure from their experiences
    in the land from whence they had just come.
There, they had experienced a bitter revelation of the fact
    that many laws were not just,
        nor were they applied equally to all citizens.

And thus, it was through them that democracy was conceived.

E. Stanley Jones, in his book, *The Christ of the American Road,*
    suggests that the American Dream,
        conceived in the Mayflower Compact,
            was born in Rhode Island,
        grew up in Pennsylvania,
became of age and was legalized in Thomas Jefferson,
    and came to embodiment in Abraham Lincoln.

Rhode Island,
    which was the smallest colony,
        gave to America the largest concept.

It was the Quakers and the Baptists of Rhode Island who declared that
    God being Father,
        all men were brothers,
            and individuals equal in the sight of God.
And, if they are equal in the sight of God,
    then they are equal in the sight of men.

Democracy was born out of the Christian faith,
    and only in the Christian faith can it be nurtured.

This democracy began to grow in Pennsylvania,
    amid the pure faith of the Quakers,
        and reached its highest expression in William Penn's principles of
government.
It remained for Thomas Jefferson to put it into words that are cherished
today.

Though it was the Christian faith that gave birth to the democratic ideals
of the young Republic,
    the beginning of the 19th Century saw the beginning of the separation—
        that was to continue for many a year—
            between the political expression of government
            and the Christian faith out of which it grew.

It is significant that Thomas Jefferson,
    who wrote his own epitaph,
        who received of his country the highest honors it could bestow,
            and who had been President of the United States,
                nevertheless had written on his tombstone:

"Here was buried Thomas Jefferson,
author of the Declaration of Independence,

of the Statute of Virginia for Religious Freedom,
and Father of the University of Virginia."

This stone that marks his resting place is eloquent testimony to the great
concepts that were born with the Republic of the United States:
    That all men are, in the sight of God, created equal.
    That in this land there would be equality of opportunity.
    That there would be just and equal laws, with liberty and justice for all.
    That the freedom to worship God according to the dictates of
    conscience was guaranteed to all.
    And that the pursuit of higher learning and education was a part of the
    inherent right of every man to life, liberty, and the pursuit of happiness.

Not until Abraham Lincoln became President did the two ideas seem to
come together again,
    for in this man,
        greater than his time,
Christianity was applied to government
    and the ideals of democracy were expressed in every utterance—
        especially the Emancipation Proclamation—
which released the slaves from their owners,
    but did not make them free.

To this day, the Negro wonders at the words of the pledge to the flag . . .
    "One nation, indivisible, with liberty and justice for all"[1] . . .
The Negro is still wondering when Lincoln's promise will come true.

The American Dream, was almost forgotten for half a century.
    Yet, when the clouds of war
        and hate,
            and famine,
                and human despair blackened the sky,
                    it began to gleam once more,

The nations of the world heard it told again by Woodrow Wilson.
And, because the people of Europe

instinctively recognized its fidelity to the original charter and conviction
of the founding Fathers . . .
and because they believed in the spiritual leadership of America . . .
they received Wilson as a leader—
with tears in their eyes,
lumps in their throats,
and a new song of hope in their hearts.

Perhaps future historians will record it as the tragedy of the 20th Century that
the vision,
the faith,
and the promises of Woodrow Wilson
were rejected by the representatives of the people.

To most of the people who come to America from over the seas,
it was the American Dream that lured them on,
that sustained them in their bitter struggles,
and that gave them courage
to uproot themselves from the Old World and seek a brighter day in the
New.

Though some came for adventure,
and some merely to escape;
though there were renegades among them,
and scoundrels then as now;
though some came for money,
seeking their fortunes,
and some of the gold with which they believed the very streets were paved . . .
most of them came to escape the clouds of war
and the chilling mists of persecution and fear.

In the gloom of despair that claimed them,
they turned to the new hope and promises of the American Dream.

Upon the Statue of Liberty on Bedloe's Island in New York Harbor, there
are these words:

"Send me your tired, your poor,
Your huddled masses, yearning to breathe free,
The wretched refuse of the teeming shore.
Send these, the homeless, and the tempest tossed to me.
I lift my lamp beside the open door."

It is because we know what it envisions,
    what it stands for,
        what it represents,
that we who have crowded the rails of immigrant ships
    have looked at the Statue of Liberty through grateful tears.

I believe I am right in this interpretation of the American Dream.

I found reassurance in the magnificent address of Judge Learned Hand,
    a New York jurist who, last May, led 150,000 newly-naturalized citizens
        in the pledge to the flag in New York City's Central Park.

Life magazine said of this address: "It is a new and solid stone in the proud edifice of American Oratory. It is not in the Webster tradition, but in the great, simple words of Lincoln:

'We have gathered here to affirm a faith, a faith in a common purpose, a common conviction, a common devotion. Some of us have chosen America as the land of our adoption; the rest have come from those who did the same. For this reason we have some right to consider ourselves a picked group, a group of those who had the courage to break with the past and brave the dangers and the loneliness of a strange land.

'What was the object that nerved us, or those who went before us, to this choice? We sought liberty; freedom from oppression, freedom from want, freedom to be ourselves. This we then sought. This we now believe that we are by way of winning.

'What do we mean when we say that first of all we seek liberty? I often wonder whether we do not rest our hopes too much upon constitutions, upon laws and upon courts. These are false hopes; believe me, these are false hopes. Liberty lies in the hearts of men and women. When it dies there, no constitution, no law, no court can save it. No constitution, no law, no court can even do much to help it. While it lies there, it needs no constitution, no laws, no court to save it.

'And what is the liberty which must lie in the hearts of men and women? It is not the ruthless, the unbridled will: It is not freedom to do as one likes. That is the denial of liberty, and leads straight to its overthrow. A society in which men recognize no check upon their freedom, soon becomes a society where freedom is the possession of only a savage few; as we have learned to our sorrow.

'What then is the spirit of liberty? I can not define it; I can only tell you my own faith. The spirit of liberty is the spirit which is not too sure that it is right. The spirit of liberty is the spirit which seeks to understand the minds of other men and women. The spirit of liberty remembers that not even a sparrow falls to earth unheeded. The spirit of liberty is the spirit of Him who, nearly two thousand years ago, taught mankind that lesson it has never learned, but has never quite forgotten; that there may be a kingdom where the least shall be heard and considered side by side with the greatest.

'And now in that spirit, that spirit of an America which has never been, and which may never be; nay, which never will be, except as the conscience and the courage of Americans create it; yet in the spirit of that America which lies hidden in some form in the aspirations of us all; in the spirit of that America for which our young men are at this moment fighting and dying; in that spirit of liberty and of America I ask you to rise and with me to pledge our faith in the glorious destiny of our beloved country.'"

There have been times when the light has almost gone out;
    times when the American Dream has faded.

We need today to make it shine again in our hearts and in our lives.

Our Government is in danger of control by corrupt party machines—
    cynical,
        ruthless,
            self-seeking,
                lovers of power and authority,
which should challenge every true patriot
    and summon all who love America here and now highly to resolve,
    in the words of Lincoln:

    "That this nation, under God shall have a new birth of freedom—
    and that Government of the people, by the people, for the
    people, shall not perish from the earth."

Our standard of values is out of focus.
    About 15% of our people own about 85% of our wealth,
        and they are far more willing to sacrifice people
            than they are to sacrifice property in this world crisis.

We pay baseball players $12,000 a year,
    and school teachers $1,200 a year.

And yet, we boast of the fact that it is from country schools,
    where men and women labor in selfless devotion,
        that most of our great leaders have come.

Movie stars and radio comedians can earn a million dollars a year,
    and those who work in essential public service labor for a bare living.

Two crises confront America today.
They are like smouldering volcanos, likely to erupt at any moment.

Should they erupt simultaneously,
   God help America.

One is the racial tensions that exist even now between the white and the
colored citizens of America,
   and between the Gentiles and the Jews.

It is a contradiction not only of the religion we profess,
   not only of the Constitution and the Bill of Rights that we boast,
but likewise, of the American Dream—
   the tradition and the purpose for which our nation was established.

The other crisis lies in the relations between management and labor.
If, at one time, America suffered from the tyranny of management,
   today the pendulum seems to have swung toward
      the tyranny of labor leaders who defy the President,
         the law,
           and the people of the United States.

There are many other things that are deeply and dangerously wrong with
America,
   but these two are acute,
      and have in them the deepest menace to all that we hold dear,
         and for which our men are fighting and dying.

All honor to the people,
   in churches,
      in various groups,
         and as individuals,
who not only are concerned about the dangers,
   but are trying with God's help,
      to do something about them.

George Washington said, in his First Inaugural Address:

"No people can be bound to accept and adore the Invisible Hand which conducts the affairs of man more than the people of the United States. Every step by which they have advanced to the character of an independent nation seems to have been destined by some token of Providential Agency."

This is the foundation upon which the founding Fathers built this country.
It is the conviction that pulses through the American Dream.
That dream must be perpetuated by us, under God.
If this dream was born of God, and I believe it was;
   if it was preserved by God, and I believe it was;
      then a great responsibility rests on us.
America may be humanity's last chance—we do not know.
But it certainly is God's latest experiment,
   and if America fails to realize her destiny,
      then the opportunity may go to another nation.

All of these empires have had their chance—
   Egypt,
      Assyria,
         Babylon,
            Greece,
               Rome—
and if you would find what is left,
   you must arm yourself with a pick and shovel . . .
      for they have crumbled, each in turn,
         and gone down into the dust.

It is conceivable that
   some day tourists might stand on what we now call Capitol Hill,
      and listen to a guide describe how on that spot stood the halls of
American Government.
He might point out two or three columns standing sentinel over some ruins and say,

"In a white house down there, the Presidents of America used to live,
    and yonder, between here and the river,
        you can see what remains of the monuments
            they erected to three of their great men."

He might tell of the great opportunity that came to this people,
    and of the chance they had—
        twice in the 20th Century—
of providing to a bleeding and blundering world,
    the spiritual leadership it needed.

Yes, that is possible.
I might even say, upon the authority of history,
    that it is inevitable-
        unless this nation is willing *to give,*
            rather than *to get;*
unless this nation is willing to share that with which God has so richly
endowed it.

For here is a Universal Law:
    As we seek first the Kingdom of God and His righteousness,
        then all of these material things shall be added unto us;
    But, if we seek something else first,
        then these other things are subtracted from us.

And that applies to the nation as well as the individual.

These are critical days in which we live.
    America is in a sober, chastened mood.

How appropriate it would be if the President
    now would issue a call for a day of national humiliation,
                            penitence,
                and prayer.
If there could be gathered together in one place, at one time,

the members of the Senate,
>the members of the House of Representatives,
>>the President,
>>>the Vice-President,
>>>>the members of the Cabinet,
>>>>>and the members of the Supreme Court . . .
all of the chosen leaders of our nation gathered together,
>to unite in a solemn assembly,
>>to acknowledge their sins as individuals,
>>>and our sins as a nation,
>>>>and to seek God's forgiveness and guidance for America . . .

to build America strong,
>to commit our nation to God—
>to rededicate themselves and the country to His will,
to the end that it may be true what we stamp on our coins—
>"In God we trust". . .

in order that this might become,
>in a truer sense than ever before,
>>God's country—

Think of the effect of this upon our fighting men in the far Pacific,
>>>>>>>>in Italy,
>>>>>>>in Germany,
>>>>>>in Holland,
>>>>>and in France.

Think of the effect of it upon our own people at home!

What a witness;
>what a testimony;
>>what a power could be turned loose in the White House,
>>>on Capitol Hill,
>>>>and in the Supreme Court,

to lead America back to the faith of our fathers;
back to the sure foundations upon which they built this nation so long ago.

> "Oh, thus be it ever when freemen shall stand,
> Between their loved homes and the war's desolation;
> Blest with victory and peace, may the heaven-rescued land,
> Praise the Power that hath made and preserved us a nation!
> Then conquer we must, when our cause it is just;
> And this be our motto: 'In God is our trust!'
> And the star-spangled banner, in triumph shall wave,
> O'er the land of the free and the home of the brave!"[2]

And so I come to my text, 2 Chronicles 7:14:

> "If my people, which are called by my name, shall humble them-
> selves and pray, and seek my face, and turn from their wicked
> ways, then will I hear from heaven, and forgive their sins, and will
> heal their land."

Are We Good Enough?

"Are We Good Enough?"

New York Avenue Presbyterian Church

Washington, D.C.

April 22, 1945

When one reads the periodicals and examines the
blueprints for a post-war world as they have been
offered for our encouragement by the spokesmen
of the contending nations in this global war,
one cannot escape the fact that they all have this on
thing in common --
        namely,
the assumption that the new order is to be an affair
of this world only....
and that all that men need for security and happiness
is jobs....
        houses to live in....
    and an industrial and political set-up well concei

A great deal of our talk has been of the better post-
houses to which we could look forward.....
                the improved radios.....
                better refrigerators....
            more efficient automobiles....
            new gadgets.....
but not very much has been said about making America
a better country......
            ourselves a better people......
    more worthy to welcome heroes home.

If there had been any doubt as to the nature of the
enemies we are fighting,
all such doubts must surely have been removed in the
evidences of bestiality.....
of such fiendish cruelty and horror that our armies
have discovered in Germany.

One great fear shared by all our correspondents who
report such atrocities is that the American public
will not believe what they write.

Our soldiers could hardly believe their own eyes....
The stenches of disease....

169

Introduction to

Are We Good Enough?

By the spring of 1945, the end of the war in Europe was plainly just weeks away. The Russians were closing in on Berlin from the east, and the American and British armies had taken virtual control of western Germany. People were eagerly looking forward to life after the war. Soon the soldiers would begin to return from overseas.

This sermon poses a probing question: What kind of America are the soldiers going to discover when they come home? What will those men find who have made such sacrifices to serve their country, who have faced death and destruction—some of whom have left pieces of themselves in Europe or the South Pacific. Will they return to a nation that is still as self-absorbed in pursuing money and things, still as racially divided, still as poorly led, with so many scoundrels in public office, as it had when they left?

Suppose God allowed the terrorist attacks of September 11, 2001, to call America to self-examination and repentance and to turn us back to Himself? If that is true, then the questions asked in this sermon of 1945 need to be asked of us today. The list of evils in our society may have changed somewhat, but the basic issues have not changed:

What kind of a nation are we becoming,
What kind of person is each one of us becoming?
Are we worthy of the sacrifices being made for us today
by our soldiers, our firemen, our policemen?
What is each one of us going to do about it?

Strikingly clear in this message is my father's insistence that real changes cannot be brought about in societies simply by political means—changing borders, trials of war criminals, or even international peace conferences.

This prophetic warning was given because a conference to set up and establish the United Nations was about to begin in San Francisco. Dad was warning his listeners that there would have to be true spiritual changes in the hearts of people before the world could expect any lasting peace.

This is as true today as it was on April 22, 1945.

Are We Good Enough?

New York Avenue Presbyterian Church

Washington, D.C.

April 22, 1945

When one reads the proposals and examines the blueprints for a post-
war world
    as they have been offered for our encouragement
        by the spokesmen of the contending nations in this global war,
one cannot escape the fact that they all have this one thing in common—
    namely, the assumption that the new order
        is to be an affair of this world only . . .
and that all that men need for security and happiness is jobs . . .
    houses to live in . . .
        and an industrial and political set-up well conceived.

A great deal of our talk has been of the better post-war houses to which we
could look forward,
    the improved radios,
        better refrigerators,
            more efficient automobiles,
                new gadgets . . .
but not very much has been said about making America a better country . . .
    ourselves a better people,

more worthy to welcome heroes home.

If there had been any doubt as to the nature of the enemies we are fighting,
    all such doubts must surely have been removed
        in the evidences of fiendish cruelty and horror
            that our armies have discovered in Germany.

One great fear shared by all our correspondents who report such atrocities
is that the American public will not believe what they write.

Our soldiers could hardly believe their own eyes . . .
The stenches of disease . . .
    of charred bodies . . .
        of unburied dead . . .
the sights of malnutrition and human misery were too much even for
seasoned veterans of war.

General Eisenhower has requested that a group of Senators and newspaper
editors be permitted to visit occupied Germany . . .
    and see for themselves what the Germans have done.
The planned program of horror was not something visited by the Germans
upon the Jews only.
The same treatment was accorded Russians,
                                    Poles,
                                        Frenchmen,
and the Dutch, the British, and the American prisoners they had captured.

There is no doubt about it.
The evidence and the testimony are undeniable.
The basic and fundamental issue of this war is what is has always been . . .
    but it is clearer now than it ever was before . . .
        namely, that we are fighting for our very lives and our homes . . .
            to hold back the reign of terror and the flood of cruelty
which the Germans and the Japanese had loosed upon the earth.

Our present safety . . .
    and our future security are both at stake.
To defend the one . . .
    and to guarantee the other . . .
        brave men went across the seas . . .
            and in the bloodiest fighting of any war . . .
                and against difficulties never before faced by any nation . . .
they are winning for us the opportunity to set up a new world order . . .
    and challenging us to see to it that such things will never happen again.

What are we doing—
                        as individuals and as a nation—
                                            to merit their sacrifices?

Are we seeing to it that they shall come back to a wholesome life,
    in a land spiritually cleansed . . .
        a land that is really like the land they dream of . . .
            the land they believe themselves defending?

As Archibald Rutledge put it in an article in one of our magazines:

    "Are we going to let them return to the old selfishness,
        cupidity,
            the swine-and-slop politician,
                the arrogant labor boss,
                    the parlor pinks of Washington,
                        the heartless employer,
                            and the ruthless business rival?"

When the first hospital ships brought back our wounded men from the
fierce fighting in Italy—
    from the Anzio beachhead,
        from Salerno and Cassino—
they docked in Manhattan after the ambulatory cases had stood on the deck

silently watching the familiar sights of the harbor . . .
   and the landmarks they had dreamed about.

Men watched the Statue of Liberty loom up out of the mist . . .
   their eyes were misty, too.

America looked good to them—it was home.

The memories of battle,
   of misery,
      of rain and cold,
         of wet foxholes and cold rations
            were beginning to fade . . .
               this was America!

There were boys on crutches,
   boys with trouser legs pinned up,
      boys with empty tunic sleeves tucked into pockets,
         boys with bandages over their eyes,
            standing there listening,
               quivering with anticipation and relief to be home.

Every sound was familiar, recognized, and hailed with delight.
And the newsboys were shouting the headlines in the papers.

It was about this time that Congress was discussing the legislation which
came to be known as the "G. I. Bill of Rights."
The headlines spoke of filibusters and debates . . .
   and a wave of strikes was sweeping the country . . .
      people were grumbling over the whiskey shortage . . .
      and lack of gasoline to drive their cars to Florida.

Hundreds of thousands of men were on strike because of jurisdictional
disputes.
It was not a question of working conditions or of living wages . . .
   but of which union would have jurisdiction over certain plants.

It was a battle for power between the A.F. of L. and the C.I.0.

Meanwhile, the plants making tanks, guns, airplanes, and ammunition were idle.

Many a man stood on the deck of that hospital ship
   and wondered bitterly in his heart:
      "Was it worth it?"
He looked down at his empty sleeve and asked himself:
      "Was it worth it?"

Things here at home have not become much better.
After three and a half years of war,
   we still have not learned the great lessons of this war.
We are still—
   some of us—
      not quite sure what the war is all about.

There are many among us who have even advocated bringing our boys home
   right now,
      and calling the whole thing off.

Such talk—
   apart from being sheer madness—
      reveals an utter lack of understanding of the issues.

It would be a gross betrayal of those who have already died . . .
   those who have suffered,
      those who have brought us so far along the road to victory
         and lasting peace.

Soldiers now returning from the fronts,
   especially the wounded,
      grave and thoughtful,
spiritually mature because of the ordeals through which they have passed . . .

do not seem to be satisfied with the conditions they find at home.

They have done their job,
   but they discover that we have failed to do ours.

They find in the land they love the same old political gangs;
   they find racial intolerance, with faults on both sides . . .
     they find scoundrels in public office . . .
      irresponsible strikers,
and the vulgar night-club air of those who have fattened on war and death.

Such men cannot help contrasting our cant,
                  greed,
              luxury,
            hypocrisy,
          lust, and avarice with
  the stern discipline,
   the heroic exaltation,
    the lean and sunburnt strength,
     the self-denial,
      the constant fortitude,
       the human comradeship and team-work,
and the high-hearted devotion of the men with whom they stormed the
beaches,
  dug their foxholes,
   brought in the wounded,
    and nursed home their crippled planes.

They wonder if chiselers, black marketeers,
                bootleggers,
                    tax dodgers,
and all other betrayers of their country are worth fighting for.

One of the intrepid leaders of the Marine Corps said after Tarawa:
  "I can never again see a United States Marine
    without experiencing a feeling of reverence."

The three surviving members of the patrol
    that stormed the volcanic height on the southern end of Iwo Jima
        and planted the American flag on its summit
            were welcomed here in Washington last week.

The Senate honored them.
It recessed and had them on the floor.
Our Senators stood and applauded them,
    shook hands with them,
        paid tribute to these brave men.

The crowd at the baseball park, likewise,
    stood and applauded when they were introduced.
One of the men was on crutches.
    It was a stirring thing to see these men whom we regard as heroes.

I do not feel worthy of such sacrifice—I don't deserve it.

I want to place this question before you:
    "Are we preparing morally and spiritually for our soldiers' return . . .
or do we think to feed their hearts as well as their bodies with bonuses and
jobs . . .
    to appease their moral hunger with money . . .
        to insult their spirits with a mere economic welcome?"

Now if we people here in America may safely do as we please . . .
    if we are able to handle our affairs without redemption from an ingrained
folly . . .
    if in our power we can rise above self-seeking . . .
    if we are able to get along quite nicely
        without contact with any power not of ourselves
            which makes for righteousness . . .
                then Christianity is irrelevant to life.

In that case,
    the Church is simply an appendage to our social and national life . . .

an extravagant diversion or cultural hobby that ought to be dissolved.

Or, at best, it is a sort of ivory tower in which peculiar people from time to time
may be permitted to take refuge from reality.

We know what Russia did to the Church.
It was stamped out as thoroughly as the regime could manage with safety,
on the ground that religion was "an opiate of the people."

We know what was done to the Church in Germany and Japan.
The Church was forbidden to bring the current statecraft
before the bar of God.
It was commanded to fall in line.

In liberal countries like our own,
and Sweden and Great Britain,
the Church was more and more regarded as a polite confraternity
of occasional pious individuals,
which had little or no social function
except to lend a tone of respectability to a culture,
man-centered,
materialistic,
and wholly worldly.

Thus, the Church was not persecuted;
it was granted every possible liberty . . .
chiefly because it was felt that the Church could be relied on
to "mind its own business."

The Church was not dangerous.
The Church—
the Protestant Church at any rate—
had no political influence.
It could deliver no blocks of votes.
It had no controlling power over education

or politics,
   or industry,
     the arts,
        marriage or divorce.

These are life's chief activities,
   and in *none of them* did the Church play any decisive part.

Modern man had become used to ignoring what might be the will of God for him . . .
   and in respect to all of these things,
     men assume their own competence.

People today are self-sufficient.
They don't need God.
They can write a peace by themselves.
They can solve their problems without any guidance or direction from the Almighty.

Unless the Christian Church rediscovers its own function,
   and begins to understand what the Church is,
     it is hardly likely to matter any more tomorrow
       than it mattered yesterday—

               or than it matters at the moment—
which is just about not at all.

The Reverend Bernard Iddings Bell, an Episcopal clergyman, has a determined conviction of the part the Church could play in the world of tomorrow.

He takes a gloomy view of the San Francisco Conference,
and he is quoted in *Time* magazine as saying:

> "There is no country today which seeks to make a peace according to the desire and wisdom of the Christ-God. We are

in for a peace of expediency. That may be the best peace we can
get, since all the nations are pagan; but at least we ought to be
honest enough to admit that such a peace is contrary to the will
of God. Will the churches say this, bravely and. honestly? That
is—one regrets to admit—exceedingly unlikely. Things being
what they are, we shall have a repetition of Versailles. One
becomes definitely bored. One has seen this show before, and it
never was a good show in the first place."

A statesman has said:

"To expect a change in human nature may be an act of faith, but
to expect a change in human society without a change in human
nature is an act of lunacy."

Will it do any good to rearrange frontiers,
  if the people who live on both sides of the frontiers still feel the same
  way?

Will it do any good to punish the war criminals
  at whose orders fiendish things were done,
    when the people who actually carried out the orders
      with the same hatred in their hearts go unpunished?

Will it do any good to bring to judgment and execution Hitler, Goering,
and Goebbels,
  without making any attempt to eradicate the doctrines
    which they have drilled into the German youth?

What will be the result of sending back to Germany the millions of
captured German soldiers, well fed, healthy, strong, virile,

                                                and *unchanged?*

And what about our own country?
How can we hope for a better country after the war is over
  unless the people who are responsible for black markets are changed?

If the arrogant, self-seeking lovers of power who control labor unions,
   and the irresponsible strikers who followed their orders are unchanged,
will they not be as big a menace during peace as they were during war?

Mere democracy is not going to help us if there is no moral regeneration.
As long as we—as individuals—remain morally unimproved,
   we shall have lost both the war and the peace.

And moral improvement begins with the individual.
   It is strictly personal.
      It is the work of the Holy Spirit.

That does not come by education . . .
   or legislation.
It is not a product of better living conditions,
   shorter working hours,
      and higher wages.
It is a spiritual thing . . .
   for only God's power can change human nature.

We here in America have been called by destiny, for the second time in
twenty-five years,
                  to assume world leadership.
It has been thrust upon us . . .
   we did not seek it . . .
      but it is ours nonetheless.

We have certain qualifications for the task.
We have the political forms,
   the means of communication;
We have the wealth,
   the natural resources,
      the skill,
         the inventions.
Materially,

and perhaps politically,
    we have left other nations far behind.

But, "righteousness alone exalteth a nation."
    Eternal law has so decreed.

Is America good enough to lead the rest of the world?

Can America achieve a moral superiority which alone
    would entitle her to call on the other nations to follow her lead?

There are many signs of a spiritual awareness among our fighting men.
Many of them are turning to their Bibles as they never did before.
Many of them are praying,
    and finding that prayer does change things,
        and give them inner peace and direction.

Many have had an experience of the nearness of God about which they may
be inarticulate,
    but not the least bit uncertain.
They know that God is,
    and that they need Him.

Moreover, many of them—perhaps most of them—really want God . . .
    want to go on feeling His nearness and reality.
Oh, it is not a conventional religion many of them have . . .
    and that is good.
But it is real,
    and it can be made into a powerful regenerative thing
that will make America spiritually stronger than she has been in many years.

When they come home,
    unless we shall have made the same spiritual progress that they have
made, they are going to be disillusioned.

They will have little patience with half measures or compromises.
They will scorn the pretenses that some people make in religion.
They will not render to the Church or to God any lip service.

It will be all or nothing.
    It will be a real consecration or none.

So the challenge before us is not so much to provide sixty million jobs,
    as important as that may be.
No daily quart of milk,
    no platitudes about this being the century of the common man,
        no full dinner pail,
            no bonuses—
nothing material is going to satisfy them completely.

We shall fail our soldier sons
    and betray their sacrifices,
unless we remember that men do not live by—

                        nor die for—

                            bread alone.

Try to see it personally in your own life.
When your husband comes home . . .
    when your son returns from overseas . . .
        when your brother comes back . . .
he must find you a better person than you were when he went away.

We should have learned something through these war years.
We must do things for them, of course.
But there is something even more important than that.

We can be the kind of people worth fighting for.

And for a start, there is this word of Christ, spoken long ago,
    for us to remember today:

"Man shall not live by bread alone, but by every word of God."

Have we learned that lesson yet?

It is not too late—but time is short.

Dedication

This is a day we have long waited for.
At last it has come....
    for us after 3½ years...

for New York Avenue Presbyterian Church
almost 6 years....

And now at last it has come.

Washington, D.C.

We can never imagine what it means to people across
the seas,
            who may take some time to realize that the war
for them is over...
as they stand looking at what had once been their homes.

V-E Day, May 8, 1945

Now the lights can go on again,
and the air raid shelters can be torn down,
    for the sirens will not wail again in the night,
and blessed sleep will once more be possible.

The guns are silent now,
and the awful carnage has been brought to an end.

There are dead yet to be buried;
        there are wounded still to be nursed back to health;
            and there are millions of people to be fed,
                            and clothed,
                        and housed again,...
if they are to go back to tilling their fields,
                        growing their flowers,
                    and making the simple things of peace.

The thoughtless will cheer...
and the unthinking will celebrate.

The announcement that came today is no occasion for
revelry,
            and yet it is sad to realize that there are
those among us who will turn to music
                            and dancing,
                                and drinking,
to mark the end of the war in Europe.

It were more fitting for us here to be gathered in
the House of God....., Lest we forget

INTRODUCTION TO

Dedication

V-E Day—Victory in Europe Day—May 8, 1945, fell on a Tuesday. The war in Europe was over, and America erupted in spontaneous celebrations! However, though Nazi Germany had been crushed, the war with Japan continued. At the time of this service, the bloodiest battle of the Pacific war was raging. Okinawa would claim 12,000 Americans dead, 36,000 wounded, and 100,000 Japanese dead. There was every reason to believe that the final defeat of Japan would require a much more costly invasion of their home islands, with American casualties in the hundreds of thousands and Japanese casualties in the millions. So, thanksgiving for the ceasefire in Europe was tempered by fears of the terrible price still to be paid in the Pacific.

President Harry Truman pled for solemnity, and Christians throughout the county held special services. At New York Avenue Presbyterian Church, my father preached the sermon "Dedication."

The central message of this sermon is set forth poignantly and eloquently: We Americans have never fought our wars just for ourselves and our own freedom. We have always contended for the God-given inalienable rights of life, liberty, and the pursuit of happiness that belong to every human being, throughout the world.

But we Americans would be guilty of the worst kind of hypocrisy if we did not first seek to live up to these standards in our own society. Rabbi Roland Gittelsohn, the chaplain giving the sermon at the dedication of the Fifth Marine Division cemetery on Iwo Jima put it in profoundly simple terms:

> We dedicate ourselves ... to live together in peace the way they fought and are buried in this war. . . . Here lie officers and men, Negroes and whites, rich men and poor ... together. . . . Among these men there is no discrimination. No prejudices. No hatred. Theirs is the highest and purest democracy.
>
> Any man among us, the living, who fails to understand that will betray those who lie here dead.

That is still true.

Dedication

New York Avenue Presbyterian Church

Washington, D.C.

V-E Day, May 8, 1945

This is a day we have long waited for.
At last it has come—for us after three and one-half years,
   for the Poles,
      the British,
         and the French after almost six years.
And now at last it has come.

We can never imagine the thoughts of the people across the seas,
   who may take some time to realize that the war for them is over,
      as they stand looking at what had once been their homes.

Now the lights can go on again,
   and the air raid shelters can be torn down,
      for the sirens will not wail again in the night,
         and blessed sleep will once more be possible.

The guns are silent now,
   and the awful carnage has been brought to an end.

There are dead yet to be buried;
   there are wounded still to be nursed back to health;
     and there are millions of people to be fed,
           and clothed,
       and housed again,
if they are to go back to tilling their fields,
   growing their flowers,
     and making the simple things of peace.

The thoughtless will cheer,
       and the unthinking will celebrate.

The announcement that came yesterday is no occasion for revelry,
   and yet it is sad to realize that there are those among us
     who will turn to music and dancing and drinking
to mark the end of the war in Europe.

It were more fitting for us here to be gathered in the House of God . . .
   lest we forget . . .
     lest we forget . . .

We do not,
   we could not forget our own flesh and blood—not for one minute—
     who are far away,
blasting a fanatical enemy out of caves,
   and tracking him down in dark jungles in the far Pacific.

No, we do not,
   and could not forget them—
      manning our fighting ships in three great oceans,
       flying their deadly missions in dangerous air,
        slugging it out with a desperate enemy.

No, our thoughts are with them—
   on lonely stations in Burma . . .

China . . .
    Iceland . . .
        from the top of the world to down under.

We remember them.

But unless the star in our window has turned to gold,
    we are apt to forget the price that has already been paid
        to win the headlines in our papers.

We are not fighting a Hollywood war—the blood is real.
The price cannot be computed.
It is not told in statistics.

The hospitals have no publicity campaigns.
    They are silent places . . .
        silent with pain.

The cemeteries, too, are silent places . . .
    only the palm trees whisper,
        or the restless seas moan on the coral beach.

In the shade of the Italian hills they lie,
    among the withered roses of Normandy,
        and by the river banks of Western Germany.

They are the dead—the fallen—who paid the price.
They are one, now, with their comrades of yesteryears,
    who did not lose their lives,
        but who gave them for all that America is . . .
            and for all she yet may be.

On the slope of Bunker Hill,
    and the bleak clearings of Valley Forge,
        they paid the first installment of the price of freedom.

The payments went on—
    Dearborn,
        Plattsburg,
           and Baltimore,
              the Alamo,
                Bull Run,
                  Antietam,
                    Gettysburg,
                      Manila Bay,
                      San Juan,
                        and Santiago,
                          Chateau Thierry,
                          Saint Mihiel,
                          and the Argonne,
Guadalcanal,
    Tarawa,
        Midway,
           Guam, and Saipan,
              Bizerte,
                Salerno,
                  Anzio, and Cassion,
                    Cherbourg,
                      Saint Lo,
                      and Carentan.

This is what we forget—
    that every right and privilege we enjoy in this good land
      has been bought and paid for in human life . . .
        every liberty, every freedom
          sprinkled with blood.

They were different, these heroes who fought side by side.
    From different parts of the country they came,
      but they loved it all.

They were not articulate, many of them . . .
  they could not have told you in so many words why they were there . . .
    it was something they felt, deep down inside—
      Catholic and Protestant and Jew.

Crouched in a foxhole,
  muttering their prayers,
    they were not so different.
Lying on stretchers . . . their blood was strangely the same.

They did not want to die . . .
They would have lived, had they a choice . . .
  but all of them believed when the showdown came,
    that what they were dying for was worthwhile.

They knew that America was not perfect . . .
  they knew that she could be better . . .
    and they wanted to purchase for her the opportunity to make patriots'
dreams come true,
  and to give her another chance to be,
    in a deep and honest way—
      God's country.

We remember them today, now,
  who lie so far away from homes in graves marked by a cross or a star,
    or the single poignant word "Unknown."

It is fitting that we remember those who lie so far away beneath a cross or a
star—
  they gave their all.

What more could they do?
  They gave the most that they had—their very lives.
    Can we ever forget that?

Since this is an occasion for rededication,
    I should like to read a sermon, which I believe
        may yet rank among the significant utterances of this present war.

It has in it the elements of great oratory and deep feeling,
there is a quality of the Gettysburg Address in it.
I shall read the sermon preached by Chaplain Roland B. Gittelsohn,
    of Rockville Center, Long Island,
at the dedication of the Fifth Marine Division Cemetery on Iwo Jima.

This sermon was part of a combined dedication held by the Protestant,
Catholic, and Jewish chaplains,
    who had shared the hardships of that terrible battle
        with the men whom they saw laid to rest.

"This is the grimmest and surely the holiest task we have faced
since D-Day. Here before us lie the bodies of our comrades and
friends. Men who until yesterday or last week laughed with us,
joked with us, trained with us. Men who were on the same ships
with us, and went over the sides with us as we prepared to hit the
beaches of this island. Men who fought with us and feared with
us. Somewhere in this plot of ground there may lie the man
who could have discovered a cure for cancer. Under one of
these Christian crosses, or beneath a Jewish Star of David, there
may rest now a man who was destined to be a great prophet . . .
to find the way, perhaps, for all to live in plenty, with poverty and
hardship for none.

"Our power of speech can add nothing to what these men
and the other dead of our division who are not here have already
done. All that we can even hope to do is to follow their example.
To show the same selfless courage in peace that they did in war.
To swear that by the grace of God and the stubborn strength and
power of human will, their sons and ours shall never suffer these
pains again. These men have done their job well. They have paid

the ghastly price of freedom. If that freedom be once again lost, as it was after the last war, the unforgivable blame will be ours, not theirs. So it is we 'the living' who are here to be dedicated and consecrated.

"We dedicate ourselves, first, to live together in peace the way they fought and are buried in this war. Here lie men who loved America because their ancestors generations ago helped in her founding, and other men who loved her with equal passion because they themselves or their own fathers escaped from oppression to her blessed shores. Here lie officers and men, Negroes and whites, rich men and poor . . . together. Here no man prefers another because of his faith or despises him because of his color. Here there are not quotas of how many from each group are admitted or allowed. Among these men there is no discrimination. No prejudices. No hatred. Theirs is the highest and purest democracy.

"Any man among us, the living, who fails to understand that will betray those who lie here dead. Whoever of us lifts his hand in hate against a brother, or thinks himself superior to those who happen to be in the minority, makes of this ceremony and of the bloody sacrifice it commemorates, an empty, hollow mockery. To this, then, as our solemn, sacred duty, do we, the living, now dedicate ourselves; to the right of Protestants, Catholics and Jews, of white men and Negroes alike, to enjoy the democracy for which all of them have paid the price.

"When the last shot has been fired, there will still be those whose eyes are turned backward, not forward, who will be satisfied with those wide extremes of poverty and wealth in which the seeds of another war can breed. We promise you, our departed comrades, this too, we will not permit. This war has been fought by the common man; its fruits of peace must be enjoyed by the common man! We promise, by all that is sacred

and holy, that your sons—the sons of miners and millers, the sons
of farmers and workers, will inherit from your death the right to
a living that is decent and secure.

"When the final cross has been placed in the last cemetery,
once again there will be those to whom profit is more important
than peace, who will insist with the voice of sweet reasonable-
ness and appeasement that it is better to trade with the enemies
of mankind than, by crushing them, to lose their profit. To you
who sleep here silently, we give our promise: we will not listen!
We will not forget that some of you were burnt with oil that
came from American wells, that many of you were killed by
shells fashioned from American steel. We promise that when
once again men seek profit at your expense, we shall remember
how you looked when we placed you reverently, lovingly, in the
ground.

"Thus do we memorialize those who, having ceased living
with us, now live within us. Thus do we consecrate ourselves,
the living, to carry on the struggle they began. Too much blood
has gone into the soil for us to let it lie barren. Too much pain
and heartache have fertilized the earth on which we stand. We
here solemnly swear this shall not be in vain! Out of this, and
from the suffering and sorrow of those who mourn this, will
come—we promise—the birth of a new freedom for the sons of
men everywhere. Amen."

Our Covenant Nation

Our Covenant Nation

New York Avenue Presbyterian Church

Washington, D.C.

November 9, 1947

The clock
It has no emotions as it tells off the days and the months
and the years.
It cannot feel the irony that we know as we come again to
another Armistice Day.

The 11th of November, for several years was a
significant date.
It was on that date, 29 years ago, that the guns were
silenced along the Hindenburg Line,
    at Mons in Belgium,
  and beyond the dark shadows of the Argonne forest.

I remember how it was marked -- how at eleven o'clock on
each 11th of November there was two minutes of silence
everywhere.
Everything stopped.
  People stood where they were, bareheaded and silent,
and a nation's remembrance was symbolized in a stillness too
deep for words.
We thought of the dead where "In Flanders fields the poppies
    blow
    Between the crosses, row on row."

We thought of the hope in which they died - that the world
might be made safe for democracy --
  that the rights of small states might be safeguarded,
that there might be set up a new world order under a c
solemnly covenanted League of Nations,
  and war itself might be ended.

"Never again", we thought, "Please God, never again."

Today, there is an irony about Armistice Day, for the hopes
to which it gave birth, have died.
There was a second World War, and the sons had to fight
over the same ground their fathers won,
  and now father and son lie together in Flanders fields.

The slogans of the First World War had been made a
mockery before Hitler invaded Poland.
Now the slogans of the Second World War - the Four Freedoms,
                        the Atlantic Charter
                and the rest - leave a bitter taste.

INTRODUCTION TO

Our Covenant Nation

The war was over. The guns were silent. Yet the iron curtain of Soviet tyranny had descended over Eastern Europe, and a new war—the cold war—had begun. The issue, as my father put it, was "between all that America says she stands for, and all that the Russians say they stand for."

And that brought up the fact that we Americans desperately needed to rediscover who we are and why we are here. The men who fought in World War II had come home from combat to another conflict—now they would have to fight for peace. Now we would find out if we could offer war-ravished Western Europe anything more than food and money. Theologian Reinhold Niebuhr stated it succinctly when he declared that to win the peace we would have to "make our cause so just that it will win the allegiance not of the comfortable, but of the insecure and impoverished."

I read these words today and I think immediately of the peoples of the third world, the impoverished and insecure in Afghanistan, Indonesia, the Philippines, Egypt, Sudan, and a host of other places. "To make our cause so just . . . " For nations to reject the terrorists' bitter agenda of hate, we have to offer them something infinitely better—hope. We must fire their hearts with America's founding vision: a society with true freedom under God, true justice under law, and equal opportunity for every person.

To do that we must rediscover God's plan for America and who He has intended us to be. Why? Because if we truly believe that these God-given ideals of life, liberty, and the pursuit of happiness are universal in every human heart, then we must show them that it is *possible,* by pressing on to continually reform ourslves into such a society. In colloquial terms, we have to put our money where our mouths are.

That is why I selected my father's Armistice Day sermon, preached well after the actual end of World War II, to be the last word in this volume. Once again, we are engaged in what I believe will become a global contest for the souls of men.

Perhaps there has never been a time in our history where it was more urgent for us Americans, both individually and corporately, to renew our national covenant with Almighty God.

Our Covenant Nation

New York Avenue Presbyterian Church

Washington, D.C.

November 9, 1947

The calendar is an impersonal thing.
It has no emotions as it tells off the days and the months and the years.
It cannot feel the irony that we know as we come again to another
Armistice Day.

The eleventh of November, for several years, was a significant date.
It was on that date—twenty-nine years ago—
    that the guns were silenced along the Hindenburg Line,
        at Mons in Belgium,
            and beyond the dark shadows of the Argonne Forest.

I remember how it was marked—
    how at eleven o'clock on each eleventh of November
        there was two minutes of silence everywhere.

Everything stopped.

People stood where they were, bareheaded and silent,

and a nation's remembrance was symbolized in a stillness too deep for words.

We thought of the dead where

> "In Flanders fields the poppies blow
> Between the crosses, row on row."[1]

We thought of the hope in which they died—
    that the world might be made safe for democracy ...
        that the rights of small nations might be safeguarded ...
that there might be set up a new world order
    under a solemnly covenanted League of Nations,
        and war itself might be ended.

"Never again," we thought, "please God, never again."

Today, there is an irony about Armistice Day,
    for the hopes to which it gave birth,
                      have died.
There was a second World War,
    and the sons had to fight over the same ground their fathers won,
        and now father and son lie together in Flanders fields.

The slogans of the First World War had been made a mockery before Hitler invaded Poland.
    Now the slogans of the Second World War—the Four Freedoms,
                       the Atlantic Charter,
            and the rest—
        leave a bitter taste.

War got rid of the Kaiser ... and brought Hitler!
War got rid of Hitler ... and brought Stalin!
Now there is talk of war to get rid of Stalin.

And what will that bring?

If the sacrifice of 300,000 Americans who gave their lives in this war is not
to be in vain,
    then a lasting peace must be secured,
      justice must prevail in all the world,
        and righteousness is the only soil in which these things can grow.

We know that—we heard it in 1918.
We believed it then,
          but did nothing about it.

The plain fact is that there can be no peace where there is no righteousness.
The Bible has been telling us that for centuries.
Our own consciences tell us the same thing.
That is God's truth.

Peace is a fruit of righteousness.
How then can there be peace anywhere in the world
    until there is righteousness among the nations?
How can there be peace in any human heart
    where there is wrong thinking and wrong living?

During the war there was a saying that "There are no atheists in foxholes."
But that was simply not true.
Putting a man into uniform,
    teaching him to handle a gun did not make him a saint.
Nor did it make him believe in God, or come to know God.

True, many a man, crouching in his foxhole,
    thought for the first time in his life about eternal things . . .
      wondered about God . . .
        prayed in his strange unaccustomed way . . .
          and found the reality that is God—
            the very presence of Christ . . .
              and became a different man.

One has only to think about Eddie Rickenbacker and his companions
    floating on their life rafts on the broad waters of the Pacific Ocean
        to recall that there were some striking experiences of conversion,
            and of men being changed under the hazards of war.

One remembers how many American flyers floating down on their para-
chutes
    to land in the jungles of New Guinea and Borneo
        discovered the work of Christian missions
            that enabled them to be ministered to by native Christians,
                who but a few years ago were cannibals.

Many a tough fighting man
    all of a sudden came to believe in missions
        and woke up to what the church has been doing all these years.

These things are true, but for the vast majority of our fighting men,
    not only were the issues of the war unknown and not understood,
        but its challenge to righteousness missed altogether.

They said they wanted peace.
But to most of them that simply meant an end to the fighting
    so that they could get back home and once again take up their own
pursuits.

It is not any exaggeration to say
    that one of the main reasons for our present difficulties abroad
        is the wide-spread idea in this country
            that the war was over when the shooting stopped.

Nothing could be farther from the truth.

The people at home,
    who were anxious for the safety of their loved ones,
                                            wanted peace.

They wanted our men safe home again, and naturally enough.
There is nothing wrong about that.
But too, they wanted peace so that once again
they could buy all the gasoline they wanted . . .
      get a new car,
          new gadgets,
              new things for comfort and luxury.

We at home wanted ease and security,
    and no interference with our personal liberties.

The fellows in the service, for the most part,
    thought of peace as the time when they would not have to "sir" anybody,
      or take any orders,
        or stand in line for anything . . .
when they could wear whatever kind of clothes they wanted,
    live their own lives,
      do what they pleased when they wanted to do it.

These things they called peace.

But actually, what we wanted was pleasure—not peace.

I have been reading a little book entitled *I Am Not Alone*.
It is a collection of letters from a fighting man of the famous Seventh Division,
    who was killed on Okinawa.

He wrote home to his parents and said: "We will win the war.
But then all will not be done.
America will need soldiers,
    warriors of the spirit,
      to fight that the hearts of men may be free as well as their lands,
        lest we have fought in vain.

"But we cannot be these warriors, not as we are.
    Because we are slaves in our hearts to our own ambitions . . .

"Sex, money and pleasure hold us captive . . .
America will need clean men and women to people a strong nation.

"But we cannot be the men, not as we are.
Because we have made the marriage vow a mockery and the family a farce . . .

"America will need some force to unite her.
But we cannot be that force, not as we are.
Because we have no faith,
    no standards,
        no destiny.
The sentimentalists say there are no atheists in foxholes.
But they are wrong.
We pray when we are afraid.
After the battle, we forget God and His laws."[2]

This fighting man, John J. Hogan,
    wrote his conviction that we were no better then than we were before
    the war.
And it was his opinion that we would be no better after the war,
    unless something in us was changed.

Well, has something in us been changed?
You judge.

We thought that things would be better,
    because after the war our assembly lines
        would once again turn out new and wondrous tools,
                                    and toys,
                        gadgets
and improvements on things to make life more comfortable and easy.

But things cannot make people great,
    nor do they make them good.

More and better automobiles . . .
  more and better washing machines . . .
    abundant supplies of nylon stockings . . .
      building materials for houses.
All these are desirable,
        but they do not make people good.

More conveniences for homes . . .
  when there is no happiness in them?
More clothes to wear . . .
  if inside your heart there is bitterness and disillusionment?
More houses for people to live in . . .
  when they don't regard marriage as a lifetime partnership?

What's the use?

The men who fought for victory will now have to fight for peace.
God knows these men fought for America.
They labored and sweated
  and went through things no human being should ever have to see or to
  know.
They suffered and fought and died.
They won the victory.

But that was not enough.

They, and we—all of us—must now fight for the peace,
  for the peace of the world.
That is the challenge that faces America today.

God seems to have placed America in a position
  where she can lead the nations of the world into a new world order—
    of international justice,
      ethics,
        and righteousness . . .

or . . .
by our hypocrisy,
   our compromises,
      our expediencies . . .
         and our own immorality,
sow the seeds of cynicism and disillusionment
   from which this nation shall never recover in a hundred years.

Are the nations going to slip back into the suicidal path of apathy,
                           materialism
                     and moral decay
that had produced two world wars in twenty years,
   eaten away the very foundations of Christian civilization,
      and turned the world into a vast slaughterhouse,
         reeking with the stench of human blood,
           and stark with hunger and despair?

Is that what 300,000 Americans died for?
A country plagued by industrial strife . . .
   betrayed and exploited by political expediency . . .
      disintegrated by one divorce for every three marriages . . .
         weakened and sickened by immorality . . .
           torn by racial and religious hatreds?

All the world knows that at the present time
   the issue is between all that America says she stands for . . .
      and all that the Russians say they stand for.

The issue is clear, and the challenge never was more keen.

Reinhold Niebuhr declared:

> "To win the ideological battle against communism, it is not
> enough to point to the crass corruptions of the original dream of
> justice which we see in the police states of Eastern Europe. It is

more important to make our cause so just that it will win the allegiance not of the comfortable, but of the insecure and impoverished."

"To make our cause so just" . . . what is our cause?

Do you know . . .
   you who fought for it overseas,
     who braved the sniper in the jungle,
      who flew through flak-filled skies,
       who waded through the mud of Italy,
        who have known the heat of the desert sun and the cold of
the North Atlantic?

Do *you* know . . .
   you who made your speeches in Congress and waxed eloquent on the
stump?

Do *you* know . . .
   who boast of your ancestry and have membership in patriotic societies?

Where is America going?

We cannot adequately answer that question until
   we understand who and what we are,
     and where we came from.

We cannot speak with any truth or realism about the future
unless we understand the past.

What have we to give Europe?
   If only grain, or money, or clothing . . .
     then we have already lost the war and the peace,
      and our own souls.

Ours is a covenant nation . . .
    the only surviving nation on earth, I believe,
that had its origins in the determination of the Pilgrim Fathers
    to establish on this continent a settlement
        "to the glory of God and the advancement of the Christian faith."

This country was founded in religious faith.
It had different expressions, to be sure—
    Quakers,
            Puritans,
                Congregationalists,
                    Presbyterians,
                        Anglicans,
                            Methodists,
                        and Baptists,
                    Lutherans,
                and Catholics of French,
        Spanish,
    and Irish stock.

All contributed to the molding of that faith
    and its free expression in this land
        where men were at liberty to worship God
            according to the dictates of their consciences.

These all believed in the equality of the individual before God,
    and that every soul was equally precious in God's sight.

They founded schools that were rooted in religion—
    Harvard and Yale were founded by Congregationalists;
        the Universities of Columbia and Pennsylvania by Episcopalians;
            Princeton by Presbyterians;
                Duke and Northwestern by Methodists;
            the University of Chicago by Baptists;
        Fordham and Notre Dame by Roman Catholics.

The hand of Providence was in the beginnings of this nation,
  as George Washington so clearly saw and stated so well
    in his First Inaugural Address.

And was it not so because in the beginning,
  this nation was established
    "for the glory of God and the advancement of the Christian faith,"
under "just and equal laws,"
  with the right to worship God according to the dictates of
conscience in religious liberty . . .
  that all should have an equal chance to
    "life, liberty, and the pursuit of happiness,"
      to provide a model for the world
        and to lead men into a better life?

At any rate, that was what John Carver and William Bradford had in mind.
That was what Roger Williams meant, and what William Penn achieved.
It was what Thomas Jefferson set down in writing that may be a little faded
now,
  but the meaning is still clear.
That is what Patrick Henry was shouting about,
  and George Mason and Richard Henry Lee.

Apart from faith in God, the history of America has no meaning.

Dr. Mackay of Princeton Seminary has said in his book, *Heritage and Destiny:*

> "The greatest spiritual task confronting us is the need to inter-
> pret for our time the meaning of the motto inscribed on each
> metal coin, 'In God We Trust' and to apply that interpretation to
> our national and international policy."

Now, a covenant nation is one that recognizes its dependence upon God
  and its responsibility towards God.

This nation was so born.

God was recognized as the source of human rights.
The Declaration of Independence says so.

A covenant nation is one which recognizes that God and His purposes
    stand about the nation and the nation's interests,
        and that the highest role a nation can play
            is to reflect God's righteousness in national policy.

Ours, therefore, is a covenant nation—
    covenanted with God in the beginning.

This does not mean that we are special favorites with God,
    although He has singularly blessed this land in which we live.

It does not mean that we can consider ourselves better than other peoples.
On the contrary, the thing that troubles us is that
we realize we are not good enough
    to accept the tremendous challenge of the leadership of the world.

But the price of world leadership is high.
For one thing, we'll have to do some suffering with the rest of the world.
We'll have to be willing to sacrifice,
                    as we have not yet done.
We have merely been inconvenienced.

We'll also have to be changed.

The call is for Christian men and women of every communion
    to become fighters for peace,
        and practitioners of righteousness.
Every Catholic and Protestant who owns the name of Jesus must fight
together
    to make America good enough to lead the world.

The forces of evil are organized on a world scale.
They fight against God,
   against religion,
     against peace.
They seek to promote confusion,
   to sow suspicion,
     and to set man against man.

All who believe in God,
   who love America,
     who cherish our heritage,
       who seek peace,
         who are sick of war,
           and who long for goodness,
             must fight for these things—
and they are worth fighting for.

In this battle, Catholic and Protestant can stand together.
We have the secret weapon of prayer—
   more powerful than the atomic bomb.
God is still upon His throne.
   He has not abdicated.

His Kingdom yet will come upon the earth.
Truth and righteousness will ultimately triumph,
   and the sacrifices of those who have fallen,
     the blood of the martyrs,
       the prayers of the faithful,
         and the tears of the saints
           will yet be vindicated.

But, we must fight for these things and be willing to agonize for them . . .
     fighting the battle in our own hearts and souls . . .
         seeking God's help to overcome our temptations . . .
         and be good . . .

and do good . . .
for the sake of peace . . .
for the sake of America . . .
for our own sake . . .
for God's sake.

This is the war that is not yet over.
We are in it.

God help us . . . to win this one too . . .
that we may not lose the other one.

In sixty seconds they had launched the life rafts....
the flimsy craft in which they were to spend three
weeks drifting on the eight-foot swells of the
Pacific ocean.

The story of the twenty-one days is a gripping epic
of human fortitude and courage.
It should be read by every American and preserved with
the sagas of brave men.

One cannot read it without tears.
It is a moving document whether the author is Captain
Rickenbacker or Lt. Whittaker.

The mere recital of the events themselves is drama,
and any attempt at imagining what they went through
must end in failure.

It is quite beyond my power to make us
over-nourished
comfortable
in armchairs by firesides
to conceive of that journey's end.

WARTIME PASTORAL PRAYERS

The sea was a glassy calm while the sun burned fiercely.
Faces
  necks
    hands
      wrists
        legs
            and ankles burned
                  blistered
            turned raw and burned again.
Drenched with the spray kicked up by the night winds,
flesh stung and cracked and dried,
    only to be burned again the next day.

They were like living creatures slowly turning on
a spit over the furnace of the sun.

Captain Rickenbacker described it thus:
  "The sea sent back billions of sharp splinters
of light; no matter where one looked it was painful.
A stupor descended upon the rafts. Men simply sat
or sprawled, heads rolling on the chest,
mouths half open, gasping."

Introduction to

The Morning Prayer
Sunday, May 28, 1944

In the Central Pacific, the Allies had taken the Gilbert and Marshall Islands from the Japanese and were planning to land on Saipan in the Marianas with two marine divisions on June 15. In Italy, strongly defended Monte Cassino had finally fallen to the Eighth U.S. Army on May 18, and the Allies had broken out of the bloody Anzio beachhead five days later, on May 23. On the eastern front, the Russians were steadily pushing the Germans back toward Hungary.

The Morning Prayer
Sunday, May 28, 1944

W e thank Thee, our Father, for the wonder of prayer that can unite us in
fervent petition,
   however much we may differ,
      from whatever different parts of the world we may come,
         out of different environments and with different needs.

Wilt Thou hear our united prayers as we humbly implore Thy guiding, guardian
power and presence
   for all those who this day are in peril on the sea,
                                                on land,
                                             and in the air,
in so many parts of the world,
   on so many different fronts,
      sharing a common danger,
         all serving together to bring about that happy day for which we
pray—
      the day when the last shot shall be fired,
         and the danger of war is over,
            and the commotion is stilled forever.

O God, Thou who art Lord of lords and King of kings,
    Thou who art the Ruler of the universe,
        Thou who art its Great Architect,
and who in the beginning didst design every part of it—
from the twinkling of the great stars to the molding of the petals of
the wayside flowers,
    from the coloring of the heavens to the tinting of the butterfly's wings—
hear us as we pray for all whom we love, who are far away from us.

If it be possible, if it be Thy will, may they be preserved from harm,
                                            from pain,
                                    and from death.

If it be possible, O God, wilt Thou enable them safely to return home,
    bringing with them the fruits of victory—
not the arrogance of conquerors,
    but the humility of men who have gone through hell and looked up at
the face of God,
        not the proud mien of men who rely upon their own strength,
            but the humble conviction that only by the power and might of God
hath victory been possible.

Wilt Thou guide at this time the leaders of our armies and navies.
Grant wisdom to all on whom fearful responsibility rests,
    that they may feel the awful importance of each human life
committed to their charge.

In the hell of conflict grant that human pity may not evaporate in the heat
of battle.

O God, we may not know what we pray for,
    we may not realize how difficult the petitions we form,
        but Thou knowest that in our hearts . . . we believe in the cause that
hath called forth so many of our men and women from their homes.

We believe in the issues that are to be decided apparently on the field of
battle.

We believe that our cause is right and just,

and in so far as its rightness and justice is in accordance with Thy will,

we pray that Thou wilt hasten the issue . . .

that lives may be spared,

that suffering and sorrow may soon be ended,

and that all Thy people everywhere may unite in a war of the Spirit,

whose weapons are love,

whose armament is prayer,

whose motive is enthusiasm and faith;

for the building up of a new world, and a new life . . .

in which this land that we love so much may in truth become God's
country—

exalted in righteousness,

and blessed, not because of its size or its strength,

but because of its faith in God.

We think today of all who in the past have given that last full measure of
devotion to all that this country means,

to all that she is,

and to all she yet may be.

As the red upon our flag reminds us of their courage and sacrifices,

may we be reminded that every privilege we enjoy is stained with blood,

still moist with tears,

and sanctified beyond our power to comprehend or understand.

May we cherish highly all the privileges that now are ours,

knowing them to have been bought and paid for in the tears and toil,

in the blood and sweat of many,

of whom we are not worthy.

O God, may Thy everlasting pity touch every trembling heart this day,

and may all who are anxious find His peace,

as they come in simple faith to pray to God.

May Thy divine love encircle and enfold each one of us,
   and may the wonderful pardon of God be shed abroad in every penitent
heart that all our sins may be forgiven and blotted out,
     that by Thy grace and guidance
       we may be more victorious when temptations come,
         and have a surer grip upon our faith,
       and a clearer view of the ideals that persuade us.

Hear the prayers of all Thy people everywhere,
     hearken unto the inarticulate yearnings of every heart in this congregation.

May the servicemen and women who have come to worship with us feel
Thy welcome
   and ours,
     and may they receive in this service at Thy hands and by Thy Spirit
such blessings as shall help them.

Give them strength,
    keep them aware of Thy presence,
      and enable them to endure whatever they may be called upon to
endure—today . . . and tomorrow . . . and tomorrow.

Humbly we acknowledge our unworthiness,
    for we have no claim upon Thy love and mercy,
save the claim that was purchased for us by Him who hung upon the tree.

In His lovely name we make our humble prayers.

Amen.

INTRODUCTION TO

The Morning Prayer
Sunday, June 4, 1944

Two days before D-Day in Normandy, the Allied invasion of Nazi-occupied France, the largest invasion force in human history—5,000 ships—lay tightly coiled at England's channel ports, ready to spring across to Normandy.

Everyone in America knew D-Day would happen soon; they just didn't know exactly when. In England, Supreme Allied Commander Dwight D. Eisenhower's nerves were stretched taut, for on him fell the responsibility to make the final decision to launch Operation Overlord. The airborne troops would be parachuted into France in the early hours of June 6, with the rest of the invasion force landing on the beaches just after dawn. But the weather over the English Channel was terrible, and the weather forecasts for June 5 and 6 were for more of the same.

As America watched and waited, this was my father's prayer.

The Morning Prayer
Sunday, June 4, 1944

Our Father, we thank Thee for the relief of the cooling breezes that bring
respite from the stifling heat.

    We thank Thee for the calm of Thy house.

        We thank Thee for the fragrance of worship

        and the rest of the Sabbath day.

We thank Thee for every gracious influence

    and every sacred memory that brings on this day new inspiration,

        that causes a resurgence of faith within our jaded hearts,

that we may learn the secrets of the quiet spirit and the untroubled heart.

Oh, may we learn how to rest in the Lord,

    to wait patiently for Him,

        to commit our ways unto Him,

           and to trust in Him,

               that He may give us the desires of our hearts.

May we learn that we cannot by worrying add one cubit to our stature,
or one ounce to our strength.

May we learn that our problems are not overcome by anxiety,
    that by fretting we cannot lessen our difficulties,
        or escape our trials.

May we discover that only as we trust in Thee and rest in Thee, can our help
come.
May our hearts re-echo to Thy promise that "they that wait upon the Lord
    shall renew their strength; they shall mount up with wings as eagles;
        they shall run and not be weary,
            and they shall walk, and not faint."[1]

Oh, rest in the Lord,
    wait patiently for Him,
        and He shall give Thee thy heart's desire.

May we now wait patiently for Thee,
    lay all our burdens down,
        and accept Thy gracious gift of peace,
            that we may feel no anxiety concerning our loved ones,
                whom we have committed into Thy hands.

As our prayers unite in intercession for them,
    scattered as they are all over the earth,
        in strange lands,
            on troubled waters,
                in vessels underneath the sea,
                    in planes high in the air,
                        we would commit them again into Thy care and keeping.

We pray that if it be possible Thou wilt keep them from harm.
If it be Thy will may they be brought safely home.

May our armed forces and those of our Allies be strengthened in righteousness,
    and our cause be crowned with success,
        that peace with justice and mercy may once again come to our
troubled blundering world.

O God, make us worthy of that for which we pray,
    that our glorious dead shall not have died in vain,
        that all for which they strove may come to pass in this good land,
            which may again under God and by His mercy
become God's country,
    humble enough,
        good enough to lead the nations of the world in the ways of God.

We would remember before Thee the homes of our congregation over which have fallen shadows.

We would remember all who are stricken this day.
Grant to them the presence and the healing power of the Great Physician,
    and to their families—
        anxious,
            troubled,
                and yet trusting Thee—
that peace and calm confidence which only Thou canst give.

Wilt Thou bless the servicemen and women who are worshiping with us at this hour.
May they have found a welcome in the House of God,
    and may they find a real sincerity of fellowship among God's people,
        that they may receive in this service the blessings they need,
            and the spiritual strength for which they came;
and that they may be attracted by the winsome appeal of Jesus Christ.

Remember every lonely heart,
    all who are homesick and discouraged,
        who feel life's frustrations weighing so heavily,
            who are not unacquainted with tears.
May they find the grace of God sufficient for all their needs.

May we altogether be humbled before Thee,
    realizing now if never before the values in life that are really important—

that life is too short for harbored resentments and nursed grudges,
    that with the world on fire we have no time for petty quarrels,
        no time for self-seeking or selfish ambitions.

So, help us to be gentle,
    walking softly with one another,
        to be understanding in all that we do and say,
lest we shall add to the world's sorrow and cause to flow one needless tear.

God help us all to be ministers of mercy,
    and ambassadors of kindness,
        for Jesus' sake.

Amen.

Introduction to

The Morning Prayer
Sunday, June 11, 1944

This prayer was given five days after D-Day—the invasion of Nazi-occupied France by the Allied forces. The landing had been an historic military success, but at a frightful price in terms of casualties. Omaha Beach was strewn with about 5,000 American men. Many more young GIs were wounded or missing.

The Morning Prayer
Sunday, June 11, 1944

Help us, our Father, to be willing to cast our burdens upon the Lord . . .
teach us how to bring our burdens to the Lord . . .
and leave them there . . .
for we are too prone to take them up again.

Far too many times we have come to Thy house with burdened hearts,
and we have found in Thy house, in the service,
something we needed for a blessing,
and yet, ere we turned again to the street and to our homeward way,
we have gathered all our worries and our anxieties,
all our fears,
and carried them home again.

Wilt Thou teach us how to let them go,
to surrender them all before Thee,
and wilt Thou reach into every heart
and take away all that oppresses and lies heavily upon it.
Take away all our fears.

Wilt Thou take away all our worries and anxieties,
    for we know that no one of us by being anxious can add one cubit to our
stature,
        or one ounce to our strength,
            nor can we in any way help the situations that cause us concern.

Teach us as children of God and believers in Jesus Christ, Thy Son,
    that worry has no place in a Christian's heart,
but only that simple faith and that calm serene trust
    that is content to live one day at a time,
recognizing that "sufficient unto the day is the evil thereof,"
    and being grateful for whatever kindness the day has brought.

But Thou knowest that many, many hearts are anxious today
    all over America,
        in Canada,
            in South Africa,
                in Australia,
                    in New Zealand,
                        in Great Britain,
                            in France,
                                all over the world,
and in each of the United Nations.

Thou knowest hearts are anxious,
    not alone concerning the fate of the venture itself,
        but concerning the safety and well being of loved ones.

We feel that our prayers are not solitary,
    but are blended in a great procession of petitions
        that has arisen to Thy throne so profusely in recent days.

We pray together that Thou, Who art the Sovereign of all the earth,
Thou, Who art the Lord and Sovereign of land and sea,
wouldst hear us as we cry to Thee for all who are in danger on land and sea,

underneath the sea,
  and above sea and land.

We pray, O God, that in the hour of their danger and their testing
  they may find Thee near.
We pray for them all,
  that they may incline their hearts to Thee and turn to Thee for comfort.
We pray that to each of them may come that knowledge of God
  that shall assure them eternal life and peace and joy forevermore.
We pray Thou wilt strengthen the hearts of the men who know Thee
  and incline unto Thyself the hearts of those who know Thee not.

In so far as our cause is righteous and just, as we believe it to be,
  wilt Thou bless it with success and crown our efforts with victory—
    not that we may strut as conquerors or boast of our strength
      but in all humility, by Thy grace and by Thy guidance
        help to bring about a new world.

With so much pain in all the world,
  and so much suffering searing the hearts of so many of Thy children,
    hear us in intercession for all the wounded,
                    the bereaved,
                  the starving,
                the homeless,
              the hopeless,
and all Thy people all over the earth who are in misery today.

O God, we thank Thee for generous hearts and brave,
  for dedicated lives that with every skill,
    and in the name of the Great Physician and in partnership with Him,
      minister to relieve pain and suffering
        and to heal the wounds of men.

Bless all the doctors and nurses—
  and if we pray especially for those who are in our armed forces

it is because our hearts are there with them.

Bless the doctors and nurses at home,
    the overworked,
        who have more to do than they can do.

We pray Thou wilt bless every effort that is made to wipe away a tear
    and ease the pain of the broken heart,
        to brighten a lonely life,
            and to extend friendship and kindness to one another.

Bless this company of Thy people,
    and the men and women in uniform who worship with us.

Help them to feel this is their Father's house,
    that they are welcome not only by Thee
        but also by us, Thy people.

May we all find that grace and strength,
    that peace and comfort that we need,
        through Jesus Christ, our Lord.

Amen.

INTRODUCTION TO

The Morning Prayer
Sunday, April 15, 1945

In the week before Sunday, April 15, 1945, President Franklin D. Roosevelt died. There was an immediate and immense sense of grief throughout America. People wept openly in the streets. FDR had been President of the United States for more years than any other man in our history. In the Depression years of breadlines, hoboes riding the rails, haggard women with tattered gingham dresses, and hungry children, he had spoken courage to the nation's fears in his "Fireside Chats." After the Japanese attack on Pearl Harbor, FDR had steeled our courage and vowed that the Day of Infamy would be avenged. Again and again, he had firmed up the nation's resolve to fight through to victory against Germany and Japan. Ordinary Americans felt he understood them; he was *their* President.

Before my father gave the morning prayer, he made the following remarks:

As we come to our time of prayer this morning,
    the uppermost thought in our minds is the great loss our nation sustained
in the untimely death of President Roosevelt.

The news of his passing stunned us all.
It seemed incredible that he should be called away from us at such a time,
    when in our human thinking it seemed that he was needed most.

All Americans grieve for him.
In every home,
    on all the seas,
        and on every fighting front,
his fellow-citizens pay homage to their fallen Commander in Chief.

As no other man of his generation,
    and few of any age,
        he inspired a high individual regard.

"My friends," he would say . . .
And somehow, that commonplace address,
   infused with the warmth of his personality,
      carried over the air and through the printed word
         into the hearts of ordinary folk
            who felt that the President was just that—their friend.

Not all the casualties of war die on the battlefield.
There can be no doubt that the dreadful responsibilities of the critical years
   through which he guided this nation exacted their toll of this brave man,
      who overcame in his own life handicaps
         that might have crushed a lesser man.

He lived to see that victory was certain.
But like Moses of old,
   his was not the mortal joy of going over into the promise land
      of the peace which, may it please God, will soon be ours.

The loss and grief are not ours alone,
   for the United Nations share with us the sorrow at his going.

He was a world figure and a world influence—but that influence will live
on.

This hour of grief and mourning must also be an hour of consecration
   in which every citizen shall dedicate himself afresh
      to the finishing of the work we are in,
         to the achieving of the victory to which our late President led us,
and to the support of him, who like Joshua, succeeds a fallen Moses.

We shall remember in our prayers that gracious lady
   who walked by his side through the years, and their children.

In a period of silent prayer, let us blend our petitions with the prayers of
America.
Let us pray.

The Morning Prayer
Sunday, April 15, 1945

Our Father in Heaven, this whole nation bows before Thee
in the presence of a strange and mighty Providence
which we cannot understand
and which brings us all to remember that Thou art God.

We felt in our hearts that the call which removed from us our late President
could not have been more untimely,
and yet we were thinking of ourselves,
of this nation that he loved and served so well.

We were thinking of the problems that confront us in this hour,
and of what he might have done in the building of the peace
for which he and all whom he commanded have striven to win.

Yet we know that Thou art God and Thou doest all things well.

When our faith speaks,
as only faith can speak at such a moment,

we say that "we know all things work together for good to them that love
God,
   who are the called according to his purpose."[1]

Though we may not understand,
   we bow before Thy judgments, which are altogether right,
      and in fervent, chastened mood,
         this nation would fall upon its knees and pray.

God, help this nation.
God, guide this nation.
God, hear this people as they commit unto Thee this land,
   and all for which it has stood through the years—
      the dreams and hopes that have shone across the seas
         and brought encouragement and new life to the troubled,
                   the persecuted,
                the oppressed,
             the hopeless in every land.

We do pray, our Father, that the vision the President saw,
   the dream he dreamed,
      insofar as it coincides with Thine own dream for this troubled world,
         may not fade or perish from the hearts of men,
but that it may continue to shine and inspire all lovers of peace,
   men of good will,
      all who seek to establish that world order
         in which there may be life and liberty for all men.

May they be guided by it,
   and inspired by it,
      and resolutely press on towards its realization.

We pray that the leaders of the nations allied with us may,
   because of our great loss,
      dedicate themselves even more completely to the seeking of Thy will
and the finding of Thy power . . .

as the great heart of this nation is touched,
  saddened,
    and filled with a wondrous pity and compassion.

Tears have filled the eyes of people everywhere,
  who in this hour of sorrow found a unity that they had not found before,
    in the sharing of grief.

Even in this hour, may our nation turn again to the God
  who hath made and preserved us a nation,
    to the God in whom we trust,
      to the God who inspired the fathers of this coun ry,
and who hath inspired all after them who walked humbly with their God.

Hear us as we pray for America,
  that the people may come to understand that
    "righteousness alone exalteth a nation,"
      and that only in God's will can peace and joy be found.

We pray for him upon whom the mantle of the highest office has fallen,
                                          unsought,
                                        unexpected.

We thank Thee that in the hour of his call he felt unworthy,
  humbled by the awful responsibility of it,
    and that he turned unto Thee in prayer
      and sought of us prayers of intercession for him,
that he might have in abundant measure the grace and the guidance of God.

We pray for our President that his mind may be illumined;
  that his heart may be made strong and his soul kept humble . . .
    that as Thou has promised to guide all who call unto Thee,
      may he seek Thy guidance every day,
        and determine, by Thy help,
to maintain the high and lofty principles upon which our nation is built . . .
  and to translate them not only into treaties and agreements,

but into international relations that shall make us into a family of nations,
    ever to dwell upon the face of the earth in peace and brotherhood.

Our Father, we think of that inner room of sorrow
    into which neither statesmen nor kings can enter,
        the inner room of a family's grief
            at the sudden loss of a husband and father.

We pray for her who walked at his side,
    for the children and grandchildren,
        for whom there was room in his great heart to love and to cherish.

We pray that they may be upheld,
    and find Thy grace sufficient for all their needs;
        that they may turn to Thee for succor and for help,
            and place their trust in Thee . . .
and be enabled in this hour of grief and parting
    to rededicate themselves in a way that shall bring into their troubled
hearts
        the joy and peace which Thou has promised.

O, our Father, we pray that the mood
    that has seized America for the last two days and nights
        may not evaporate and thoughtlessly be laid aside.

May we never recover from the feeling of our helplessness and our need of
Thee.
Grant that America may never again forget it,
    but that we,
        united as a people,
            may seek to know and to do Thy will.

We think of other sorrows,
    less public but no less keen,
        that have come into humbler homes,

and have touched hearts that ache in the same way,
    and eyes that weep the same kind of tears.

We pray that the Holy Spirit,
    who must be so busily engaged these days in binding up broken hearts,
        will not forget those whose names we whisper.

We think of so many who suffer pain, who explore all its vast treasuries.
    O God of mercy and compassion, have pity upon them,
        and Thou, Christ, who art the sympathizing Jesus,
            wilt Thou walk beside them in their trouble.

May Thy blessing rest upon all worshiping with us in the uniforms of Service,
    that they may find in our worship that which shall inspire,
        and be to them chart and compass,
            that which shall keep them strong in temptation,
                    resolute in duty,
                girded with courage,
and determined so to love that the fruits of victory shall not wither . . .
    and that having won the war by Thy help,
        we shall not lose the peace.

So may there come a blessing to each of us,
    a pardon for all we have done amiss,
        for every sin and transgression,
            for every impulsive act which we now regret,
for every thoughtless deed which we would recall if we could,
    for everything said that we would take back.

God, forgive us all, and help us to be better men and women,
    that this land may continue to be blessed of God,
        and may become in a new way God's own country,
            and we, God's people.

So might it be, by Thy Spirit and Power.
Thou who hast made us and preserved us a nation,
    make us and preserve us as Thy people.

Through Jesus Christ, our Lord.

Amen.

INTRODUCTION TO

The Morning Prayer
Sunday, April 22, 1945

This prayer was given on the Sunday before the opening of the historic conference in San Francisco which would create the United Nations. The hope was that it would create a forum which would prevent future world wars.

The Morning Prayer
Sunday, April 22, 1945

We know, our Father, that we must come just as we are,
but we know that we *dare* not,
we *shall* not go away just as we came.

For Thou hast promised that Thou wilt receive us,
wilt pardon us,
wilt cleanse us,
and wilt give to us Thy Holy Spirit . . .

that we shall go back to the places of our responsibility and our duty changed—
no longer what we were when we came,
but renewed with a new vision of Thyself . . .
with a new sense of Thy presence,
with a new hunger and thirst after righteousness . . .
a new consecration to be Thine.

We pray that this change may come upon us now,
that we may not go away with empty hearts.

Thou knowest whence we came and why.
 Thou knowest all about us,
   and Thou art able now, in the twinkling of an eye,
     to meet all our needs.

May we be receptive.
 May we be seeking, remembering that if we seek we shall surely find,
   if we knock, it shall be opened to us.

We pray not for ourselves alone;
 we pray for all who need Thee this day,
   even the whole world.

We wonder in our hearts if the world ever needed Thee more than now.
We wonder if there ever was a time when the nations of the world
 needed the counsel of Almighty God more desperately.

As we pray for the conference to open this week,
 there may be doubts that tug at our heart strings;
   there are fears that whisper.

It is through faith we know that Thou art still the Lord God Omnipotent,
 and reigning over all the earth,
   that Thou wilt hear the prayers of people everywhere,
     in whatever tongue they speak.

We know that Thou art not disinterested in the affairs of men,
 but tremendously concerned about what they do and decide.

Thou too wilt be there, the Unseen Delegate, there in their midst.
He who bore the crown of thorns,
 and whose hands still bear the print of the nails, will be there.

May they who sit around the tables feel His presence;
 may they know of His nearness;

may they be conscious in all that they say or think or do,
 that One stands watching and waiting.

We pray, our Father, that this opportunity
 which Thou has given us again in this century may this time be seized,
  that it may be used for the framing of such a peace
   that Thou wilt be able to bless it,
    that it may assure such a new world order,
that Thy spirit shall prevail on all that is said and done and attempted.

If there are proud hearts, make them humble.
If there are hard and bitter hearts,
 make them soft and kindly.
If there is desire for revenge,
 transform it into desire for righteousness.
If there is jealousy and suspicion,
 may it be made into trust and confidence.

O God, grant that this opportunity purchased by blood,
 obtained by suffering and heroism,
  may not be lost,
   that the dead shall not have died in vain . . .
and that they who bear in their bodies the scars of battle
 may yet come to regard them as medals,
  may come to look upon them with pride
as they think of what they purchased.

We know in our own hearts, our Father,
 that their sacrifices will be mocked unless we become changed,
  different men and women.

Remind us that we were redeemed by the sacrifice of our Lord,
 and redeemed again and again by Thy grace and mercy
  in that Thou has made and preserved us a nation
   and blessed us beyond our deserving,

beyond our comprehension.

May we live as a redeemed people;
    may we act as the recipients of God's richest mercy,
       and create, even as the founding fathers intended,
          a nation under God
in which there shall be life, and liberty, and the right to seek happiness for
all men—
    created equal in the sight of God, and therefore brothers.

Help us to make that dream come true,
    and in our homes day by day,
       in office and street and school,
so to live that Thou shalt be able to bless us,
    and to bless the nation for which we pray.

We thank Thee for the safe return of loved ones from overseas.
We thank Thee for the preserving grace that hath kept them from harm.

And, as they come home to us,
    may they feel the sincerity of our prayers
       that we may be worthy of the sacrifices they have made . . .
          that we may have matured spiritually as have so many of them . . .
             that out of the dark years through which we have passed there
shall come a bright and a good day.

All these things we ask in the name of Jesus Christ, our Lord.

Amen.

INTRODUCTION TO

The Morning Prayer
Sunday, May 13, 1945

The war in Europe had been officially over for five days, but the Japanese would hold out on Okinawa until its commander killed himself on June 22. Atom bombs would be dropped on Hiroshima and Nagasaki in August, convincing the Japanese government that further resistance was futile. The final surrender ceremony would take place on the battleship *Missouri* in Tokyo Bay on September 2. Because of the surrender of Germany, President Harry Truman had officially called for Sunday, May 13, 1945, to be a Day of Prayer.

The Morning Prayer
Sunday, May 13, 1945

Dear Lord and Father of mankind, forgive our foolish ways."

How foolish our ways are and have been, Thou knowest.
Grant that we may now realize how foolish indeed
   are the ways of men who seek not the guidance of God.

"Reclothe us in our rightful minds; in purer lives Thy service find, in deeper reverence praise."

Oh, wilt Thou reclothe us now in our rightful minds,
   that we may be able to think clearly,
      to speak honestly,
         and to do justly—
that there may be built in the hearts of this people
   that "righteousness which alone exalteth a nation,"
      and in this land a concern for all mankind . . .
         a government of liberty and justice for all,
           an integrity of purpose,

and a warm compassion
that shall steady and support those in need.

Guide and inspire the nations of the earth
    as they seek to rebuild
        what hatred and violence and falsehood and despair have destroyed.

We unite our prayers with the prayers of a whole nation,
    summoned by the President to the throne of grace.
May we, like him, fall upon our knees,
    and beseech Thee to hear the cries of our people.

Hear and save our nation,
    save us from arrogance,
        from pride and boasting,
            from the lust that comes with victory—
                the lust for domination,
                    and lust for selfish gratification.

O God, save this nation from the perils of the peace,
    no less than the dangers of the conflict.

Save her now from the dangers of victory, and,
    insofar as our cause is just—
        as we believe it to be—
            hasten the end of the conflict on the other side of the world, where
hatred is spilling like a hellish flood to engulf the whole earth.

Grant, O God, that there may speedily come a cessation
    of all that drives man against man
        and brings sorrow to the hearts of people everywhere.

Wilt Thou reveal Thy will for America,
    that she may realize her destiny and place in Thy plan for the world
Thou hast made.

May we understand
  that freedom can exist nowhere unless it exists everywhere,
    that the few cannot enjoy liberty unless it also be available to many,
and that whatever threatens human life and integrity across the sea
must also threaten them here.

On this day of hallowed memories,
  on this day with all its connotations of love and devotion—
    the deepest things in the hearts of men—
we pray that Thou wilt make us grateful for love and care
  and for those in the past who have made us what we are.

We thank Thee for mothers' love and devotion,
  that suffered long and was kind,
    that sought not its own,
      that was not puffed up,
        that endured, waited, prayed, hoped, and dreamed.
We thank Thee for that love,
  and pray that we may be more worthy of it,
    and may so live as to grant their hearts' desire
      when they seek for us not fame,
                          or position,
                or riches,
but goodness and integrity and kindness,
  and qualities that are imperishable,
    that nothing can destroy.

O, our Father, wilt Thou bless this congregation,
  the people who are gathered to worship Thee.

May they find that which shall sustain and guide them.
May there come the blessing they need.
May it have been good for us to be here.
May the batteries of our souls become strong and active
  as we give ourselves anew to follow our Lord and Master.

Help us to be better men and women,
   kindly affectioned one to another,
      forgiving one another,
         even as Thou for Christ's sake art willing to forgive us all.

So, bless us and keep us in the name of Him Who loved us,
   and gave Himself upon the Cross,
      even Jesus Christ, our Lord.

Amen.

The Morning Prayer
Sunday, November 18, 1945

This prayer was given at a time when many of the servicemen and women were returning from overseas following the conclusion of World War II. Eager to leave the horrors of war behind, America's brave sons and daughters looked forward to a future of hope, peace, and prosperity.

The Morning Prayer
Sunday, November 18, 1945

We know, our Father, that Thou art the giver of love.
We know that love is indeed a gift.
Help us also to know that we are responsible for what we love.

We join in prayer that we might come to love Him who loved us,
    and loves us still . . .
who loved us even as He toiled His way up Calvary's Hill . . .
who loved us even as He hung upon the Cross . . .
who loved us even when reviled and spat upon . . .
    even when the lash fell across His back.

For a love like that what can we offer?

Help us, we pray Thee, with our love,
    however poor and weak and faint,
        to love Him Who first loved us.

And, that we might love Him,
    O Lord, may we see Him.

Give to us this morning a new vision of Jesus Christ, our Lord,
   and give to us a new sense of His nearness,
      that we might think of Him not as a distant, far-away being,
         not as a robe-clad figure who walked the earth many years ago—
but let us feel Him now as the Man of the Ages,
   still walking the city streets,
      still tapping men and woman on the shoulder,
         still plucking the careless sleeves,
            still whispering in deaf ears,
still leaving the tracks of bleeding feet along the ways of men.

Turn our love from the selfishness of loving ourselves,
   and set our affections on things above, O God,
      that in loving the Good and True—
something of God, something of the Good and True—
might be reflected in us who love Him.

Make us to love Christ,
   that some of His beauty and grace may linger upon us.

We have come in the beauty of this Thy day,
   seeking refreshment for our souls,
      seeking new power and strength for the batteries of our spirit.

We have come, some of us,
   from the dark forests of pain;
and some of us from wandering in the dry, parched deserts of disappointment;
   some of us from the lanes of sorrow,
      lined with the weeping willows of broken hearts;
and some of us from wandering in a maze of perplexity,
   with decisions lying upon our minds,
      and choices clamoring in the corridors of our hearts;
and some of us, wearied with the routine of life
   until the iron of its monotony has eaten into our very peace;
and some of us, careless and indifferent,

unconscious of divine presences,
    frustrated because we see no purpose in our lives
      and no direction in our going;
and some of us, with joy and new hope beating high within us,
    seeking Thy blessing, if it may be, upon our endeavors,
      not that we would bind Thee to our will,
          but that we would thank Thee for the revelation of Thine,
          and thank Thee for the joy that comes from walking in it.

We bring unto Thee the servicemen and women worshiping among us.
Thou knowest whence they have come,
    the dangers from which they have emerged,
      dangers not told by ribbons on the breast,
        nor yet by scars on the body,
but rather by the shadows on the soul which Thou alone canst see.

We thank Thee for the safe return of all who have come home.
We pray that they who yet may serve may have grace and patience—
    and with deep thanksgiving that they have been spared—
may dedicate themselves, with all their comrades
    to the building of that new world for which so many died.

So, our Father, we pray the simple prayer: God bless us everyone,
    and bestow upon us during this hour of prayer the blessings we need
most.

We know not how to pray as we ought.
We rejoice in Him Who makes intercessions for us,
    Who pleads the wounds in His hands,
                    His feet,
                    His side.
Since He pleads His finished work on Calvary,
    and since we have accepted that gift of salvation,
      hear us for His sake.
O God, give us the grace "to finish the work that we are in,

to do the right as Thou hast given us to see the right,
    and to do all that may insure and establish a just and lasting peace
        in this nation and among all nations."[1]

And we pray that "government of the people,
      by the people,
        for the people,
          shall not perish from the earth."[2]

Make us ever mindful of our great heritage,
    and make us here highly resolve to dedicate ourselves to nobler living,
      in order that this country that we love so much
        shall become God's own country.

All these things we ask in the lovely name of Jesus,
    and for His sake.

Amen.

Notes

Why Should God Bless America?
1. Abraham Lincoln, "Proclamation Appointing a National Fast Day," March 30, 1863.

Rendezvous in Samarra
1. In the movie, *A Man Called Peter*, Richard Todd preaches a slightly different message, entitled "Go Down Death." The contents of the messages are essentially the same, but the stories and illustrations are different. This sermon, "Rendezvous in Samarra," is what Dad actually preached at the academy on December 7, 1941.

Why Does God Permit War?
1. Rudyard Kipling, "Recessional," June 22, 1897.

The Greatest Adventure
1. Isaiah 55:6–7

A Text from Lincoln
1. Herbert Agar, *A Time for Greatness* (New York: Little, Brown and Company, 1945).

The Armor of God
1. Isabel H. Barr, "Spring in Scotland."

The American Dream
1. The phrase "under God" was not added to the Pledge until 1954.
2. Francis Scott Key, "The Star-Spangled Banner."

Our Covenant Nation
1. John McCrae, "In Flanders Fields" (1919); poem poignantly describing scenes of World War I.
2. John J. Hogan, *I Am Not Alone* (Washington, DC: Mackinac Press). Used by permission.

The Morning Prayer: Sunday, June 4, 1944
1. Isaiah 40:31.

The Morning Prayer: Sunday, April 15, 1945
1. Romans 8:28.

The Morning Prayer: Sunday, November 18, 1945
1. Paraphrase from Abraham Lincoln's Second Inaugural Address.
2. From Abraham Lincoln's Gettysburg Address.

THE INSPIRING STORY OF ONE MAN'S JOURNEY OF FAITH

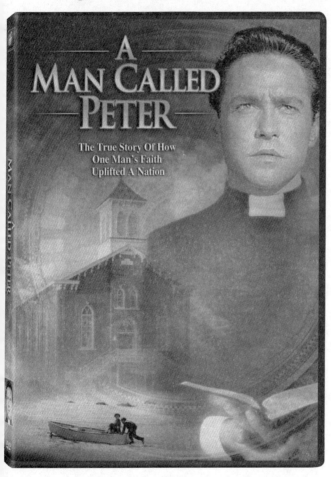

BRING HOME
THE
INSPIRATION
ON DVD

A touching story about faith, inspiration and love, this Winner of the 1955 Academy Award® for Best Cinematography is a compelling film that follows Scottish minister Peter Marshall's early beginnings and ultimate rise to become Chaplain of the U.S. Senate. Available on DVD from Twentieth Century Fox Home Entertainment including bonus features, theatrical trailer, an audio sermon by Pastor Marshall and much more.